To Manoj —
you brighten my world,
and you're the only place I ever want to spend all my time.

To Mom, Papa and Tina —
you taught me that love gives time its meaning,
and that a bright life is one lived fully, together.

Contents

Introduction

WE HUMAN BEINGS ARE UNIQUE. WE ARE BLESSED with an absolutely infinite sense of imagination but with absolutely no time to translate that into reality. We are blessed with unbridled thoughts but constrained by our ephemeral bodies. The brevity of human life is a sobering reality that often escapes us as we are glued to our screens. But we suddenly find immense value in our time when we have to spend an ten extra seconds heating our food in the microwave or wait in a slow-moving queue at a café.

This dual approach to time—we are simultaneously completely uncaring or even blissfully unaware about our limited time on Earth but are extremely concerned and even irritated by mere seconds passing without our control—is hardwired in all of us. We want to save the next second but are comfortable with flowing with the daily routine in no particular direction. Be it someone stuck in a Bangalore traffic jam or trying to board the Mumbai local train to reach home early, everyone wants only one thing— more time. But we are not particularly bothered about what we do with this 'more time'.

Our relationship with time is ambiguous. We treat it like a thing that we can 'have'. The most frequently used excuses we use go like this, 'I can't meet you this month because I don't have time' or 'I really want to learn to play the guitar, but I don't have any time at all'. Maybe we need to pause and think, who has time? Is time really a thing that we can possess? Like money, the other scarce resource, is it something that we can gather, hoard, invest and save for future use?

This flawed thinking extends to the world of work too. In a recent surge of corporate patriotism, two of India's prominent business figures proposed marathon working weeks as the path for the nation's economic progress. Narayana Murthy, co-founder of Infosys, advocated for a seventy-hour working week, and not to be outdone, S.N. Subrahmanyan, chairman of L&T, took it a step further, suggesting a ninety-hour one, essentially making work the only life one has.

Murthy urges Indians to 'work hard' to contribute to the nation's progress. While the intention is noble, a seventy-hour working week translates to working twelve hours a day, six days a week. Imagine this relentless grind paired with the constraints of the salary of an entry-level IT job. Subrahmanyan even commented, with what might be perceived as insensitive humour, that employees should prefer time at the office over personal moments, questioning what they do at home! This perspective trivialises the importance of personal relationships, rest and the need to recharge oneself. It also raises concerns about the flaws of the hustle culture that is sometimes celebrated at Indian corporate houses. Do we value output over well-being, the count of work hours over meaningful work, and busyness over productivity?

At the heart of this lies a fundamental misunderstanding of the concept of time. These business leaders are equating the measure of time, the clock, with time itself. It is like equating potatoes with the hexagonal weights used to weigh them. But can one consume the iron weights instead of the potatoes? Rather than seeking ways to work smarter, the Indian corporate glorifies working longer, equating exhaustion with ownership, hustle with dedication, and hours spent with progress made. The real question is not 'how long can you stare at your wife?'; it is 'how do you find meaning in the time you spend, whether staring or working?'. Those pushing for longer working hours may feel they are going to maximise output, but in reality they are asking us to trade away the one resource that we can never reclaim—time.

Imagine a game of cricket with no time limits. Would we still enjoy such a game? For every run a team scores, the opposition can make another. A six would lose its thrill because countless more could follow. Would such a game be worth playing? The intensity, urgency and the very essence of the game come not from the players or their energy or the leaderboards but from the fact that the time of the game is limited. Without an endpoint, the game would lack all meaning or excitement. It is the constraint of time that makes every moment count.

Celebrated German philosopher Martin Heidegger extended this thought to life itself. Just as a cricket match exists only within its allotted time, our existence is bound by the time we have. The metaphor follows beautifully. There is no external clock that is ticking for us, and no external timekeeper is keeping the score—we are our own time. The clock is just a measurement tool; it is not time itself. While the clock will continue to tick forever, our own time will eventually run out.

Hence, for every decision and action we take, the ultimate currency we pay is not money; it is not even effort, but time. By choosing to spend our time in one way, we are rejecting all the other ways in which we could have spent it. This is the opportunity cost of time, where, by choosing one path, we forgo all others. The choice of spending time is irreversible. It is definite. And that makes it meaningful. Time adds meaning even to the choices we don't end up making; hence, we feel the pressure to make the best choices every single time. The price tag of each action is time, and the commodity being traded is our life itself.

But this is not a new struggle. From the ancient philosophers like Plato and Aristotle trying to unravel the mysteries of time to today's knowledge workers striving to manage it to the best of their abilities, the concept of time has always fascinated and yet eluded us. From the timeless wisdom of the ancient civilisations, teachings of the Gita and Zen Buddhism to the mind-bending concepts of modern thinkers like Heidegger and Schopenhauer, from physicists like Newton and Galileo to the epic personification of 'main samay hoon' from B.R. Chopra's *Mahabharat*, humanity's quest to comprehend and tame time has spanned millennia. But why are we so fascinated with time? Why do we seek to understand it? More importantly, why do we always feel the need for more of it?

The answer lies perhaps in the fact that all things in our lives not only find meaning through time but also authenticity. The word 'authentic' comes from the morbid ancient Greek 'afthéntis', which means 'murdering with one's own hands'. To be authentic, one needs to take a stand and make an irreversible choice, one that metaphorically kills all other possible choices. To be authentic and meaningful, something has to be final, irreversible. Take something as simple as the food my mother makes. For me, it is far more meaningful, not to mention tasty, than a meal purchased from a restaurant. She has put in effort and, more importantly, her time, which she will never get back. That sacrifice gives it value and meaning for me. Time is the currency she traded when she made the food herself, instead of using money as a currency and buying food instead. Of all the choices she could have made, she chose to be in the kitchen for that particular period and made food. Had life been infinite, that choice would have been immaterial, but since it is finite she had to choose to kill all the other choices for that time.

Authenticity is making the choice of spending your finite time, your most valuable investment for others or for oneself, and that is what makes it meaningful and valuable. However, as soon as the authentic currency of time is exchanged with a different one, like the currency of the clock, money, effort or technology, its value, authenticity and meaning get lost. The clock is both a measurement instrument and the language of time. Since we all are 'our own times', the clock is the language we use to communicate with each other. The language of the clock divides time into hours, minutes and seconds. And it is precisely this division that is the backbone of the world economy. This segmentation of time has allowed it to be sold and purchased in the labour market and has enabled the exchange of the authentic currency of our time with the inauthentic currency of money. While our time is our own, the clock's time or—as Heidegger called it—'world time', is everyone's and no one's. Money, too, is a world good and belongs to everyone and no one. For this reason, investing money is not as authentic as investing one's time. The value of time far exceeds the value of anything else.

Today, technology, the internet and the digital world have made us more disconnected from our own time. These tools operate on the 'world time' and take us away from our personal moments to a shared, impersonal, inauthentic world; our minds hijacked to surf world time, the cyber world that belongs to everyone and no one. Today, as we find ourselves immersed in this reality of world time, the struggle to manage our time is amplified. With Instagram reels and distractions competing for our attention, we find ourselves unable to keep up with the pace of modern life. From the constant pings of WhatsApp messages to an onslaught of emails and puppy videos, from making ends meet at work to giving attention to our kids and loved ones, it often feels like this precious time is slipping through our fingers with nothing to show for it.

In this whirlpool of activity, we have little control over our time and sometimes find our own lives passing by us. One day, we were kids trying to pass the time on long summer afternoons, and the next moment we were running against the clock, trying to meet some unattainable deadlines. How many times have we questioned ourselves: where did the days, weeks and even years go? Weren't we bumbling teenagers just a few years back? Where did the hopeful youth go, and what opportunities did we miss? This feeling of disorientation is universal. We feel untethered, drifting with no clear sense of direction or purpose.

Precisely these moments of surprise and reflection are the first step towards redefining our relationship with time. Instead of being helpless spectators and watching our lives unfold, we can take a much more active role. We can take charge of consciously choosing and spending our time with intention. But to even begin doing that, we need to decode who we are and what we want with our limited time on Earth. We need to understand our 'authentic' self. What gives us meaning and what do we value? Why do we want more time? What would we do differently with it? How different would our life be?

This book is the first of a series aimed at answering these questions. The Bright Life Tookit series has been designed with the vision to help people lead a Bright Life—a life that's enriched, more fulfilling and deeply purposeful. This first book in the series, *The Time Energy Toolkit*, focuses on understanding time and engaging with it with intention, because time is both the foundation and the constraint. It aims to guide us towards our purpose and get us in touch with the rhythms of our body's energies. The book attempts to give us a toolkit to make the most of our time on Earth.

The subsequent books in the series will delve deeper into self-discovery, helping readers uncover their truth and motivations, and manage their unique selves and interactions with others. Once we understand ourselves better, we can apply that knowledge to become better leaders in the corporate world and, more importantly, better human beings leading a Bright Life.

At its core, the Bright Life philosophy is about living with purpose, verve, energy and intention. It is about being our authentic selves and the source of Brightness for ourselves and all others. It is about making conscious choices that align with our deepest values. A Bright life is not just about professional success or maximising productivity but creating a life that is deeply satisfying and meaningful on all fronts. The series is designed to equip you with actionable, practical toolkits to unlock the pathways to live that Bright life.

With this book, we will attempt to reimagine and decode our relationship with time. More than just providing you with a set of techniques to make your time truly matter, the toolkit aims to develop a deeper understanding of who you are, what drives you, when you are at your best and when you need to take a break to recharge.

The book is filled with multiple experiments and exercises, and I urge you to try and see what works best for you. We will begin this journey by establishing a baseline, an understanding of your current relationship with time. With a strong foundation of awareness, we will then attempt to understand where and in what direction you want to steer this relationship. Once we fix our North Star, we will explore exercises to strengthen, enrich and nurture this relationship.

We will understand the Indian sociocultural context and how we, as Indians, perceive and engage with time. Drawing from these relatable examples, we will explore practical strategies and experiments to achieve four main objectives: first, understanding who we are, both our physical and aspirational expressions; second, what we want with our time on Earth; third, how we find more time or reclaim it from where we are spending it; fourth, how we make the reclaimed time meaningful and intentional. This book is not about enhancing productivity—it aims to guide you towards purposeful productivity and familiarise you with your own time and energy systems. This book seeks to not make more time for you; it aims to help you be authentic and understand that you are time!

We begin by examining who we are and what we want to do with our time here on Earth. With the help of some experiments on multiple time scales, we will work on defining our purpose, finding our core and discovering our North Star. We will go deep into our past and, on that foundation, attempt to build a clear vision of our future relationship with time. This North Star will then help us align our decisions and prioritise our actions to what truly matters to us.

We will then listen to the internal rhythms of our body, attempt to decode the signals that our brain and body send to manage our energy, and are develop a deep understanding of how intricately our energy and our time are connected. We will take the help of some concepts from science and neurobiology to manage our energies and thereby manage our time.

We will then deep-dive into why we currently lack time. Why do we constantly feel overwhelmed by deadlines, unable to prioritise what to work on? Why do we find ourselves procrastinating or deferring our tasks to the following Monday and end up choosing Netflix over work? Only with this awareness can we begin working towards any meaningful change.

With this understanding, we will then try to find time, and work on making that time matter. We will reevaluate how we spend our hours and identify what activities to focus on. We will understand the science and art of focus. We will explore changing our schedules to adapt to our bodies' internal rhythms to help us derive the most of our time and make our day brighter.

This book is a toolkit designed around experimentation and reflection. Always have your pen and notebook handy to try out the experiments suggested. Make your own notes, models and schedules, and see what works best for you. Keep the reading experience interactive to draw the most out of the book. Since we are all unique, not every technique will suit everyone. So, it is essential to experiment and find what suits your unique requirements. Reflect on your experiences, adapt what fits your needs, and cultivate a rhythm that feels natural and sustainable, one that feels in sync with you.

In essence, this book is a guide to self-discovery, a guide to decoding time and, with some experiments, understanding how we can make it matter. This book attempts to illustrate that no one can master time because time is not a thing to be owned or a possession to be spent.

To be human is to exist beyond the physical and be alive in our spirit, conscious of ourselves and of the gift of our limited time on Earth. To be aware of this truth is to be aware of what it means 'to be'. To be aware of what it means to be is to know why we exist, what the purpose of our existence is, what we do, authentically, with our time on this planet, and how we use this time and our energies best. That is the 'being' in 'human being', and this book is a step towards decoding it.

By the end of our journey together, I hope you will have a comprehensive toolkit to understand yourself, your body, your energies, your deepest values and aspirations, your fears and your drivers, and, armed with this information, work towards making your time matter. This will help you understand that your time is indeed who you are, which in turn will enable you to live a fulfilling, purposeful life.

Section 1
Discover Your Purpose

CHAPTER 1

Purpose and Personality

REMEMBER OUR BIRTHDAY PARTIES AS KIDS? APART from the eager anticipation to open the gifts received and unbox happiness, we were also frequently attacked by ubiquitous uncles and aunties: 'Who do you want to be when you grow up?' 'Astronaut!' some of us answered. 'Doctor!' 'Movie star!' 'Shopkeeper!' Our answers were many and varied.

These early dreams have their roots in our natural curiosity and the influence of our surroundings. The stories we hear, the books we read, the movies and TV programmes we watch, the people we admire—all shape our desired future. At this age, our hopes are unbounded and our dreams limitless, untouched by the constraints of practicality. We have no care for financial feasibility, societal approval or even the physical possibility of the dream. Pure passion, energy and excitement—that's all there is! For the young, the world is indeed their oyster!

However, as we grow, our answers to this question keep evolving. We explore and understand our likings, strengths and weaknesses better, and make different choices than what our younger selves dreamt about. When we're older, our parents, even with their best intentions, may impose their aspirations on us. Societal expectations and financial implications require us to continuously recalibrate. So far as this evolution of our dreams is an organic process driven by our choices, we take it in our stride and benefit from it. If the change is enforced by external factors like finances, peer pressure or parental expectations, we may find ourselves on a path we don't like, that doesn't align with our natural inclinations. We may then be unable to give our best to a journey that cannot give us lasting happiness.

In the latter case, if we do not achieve lasting happiness, we find ourselves chasing it. We mistakenly believe it can be found in achieving a position, the next big promotion, the next workplace success, the next big award! We have conversations on event-based successes with ourselves. 'I will be the happiest person if I get promoted the coming year!', 'Once I become a doctor, I will be really happy!'. But we forget that the happiness achieved even with the most astronomically significant event or success will still be transient. We will celebrate it for a day or a week and fall back into our default state, wondering what's next.

This transient happiness from chasing milestones or achievements keeps us running the rat race. Lasting happiness requires something more profound. It must be something other than a race towards a single position, a designation or a goalpost. After achieving it, we shouldn't be left rudderless. It most certainly cannot be something we can one day reach or someone we can be, and feel that there's nothing more left in life.

From childhood, we are being told a big fat lie. In primary school, we are told to keep our heads down and study, and life would be better in secondary school with more freedom. And the lie continues, first the tenth standard, then the twelfth standard examinations. We are asked to study for competitive examinations and secure admission into a good college, after which life is supposed to be golden. We are given the hope of getting placed in a well-paying job and of living like a king if we study well in college. Once you join the corporate world, the race for promotions and power begins, never to end.

The goalpost keeps shifting, and we keep running the endless race, in search for the ever elusive lasting happiness.

The problem with this approach is that we are so focused on reaching our next goalpost that we completely forget that what matters more is the act of running. Life is not a magical destination, no Shangri-La that, if reached, will ensure eternal happiness. It is the journey itself. The best we can do is find where we want to go and strive to move in that direction. It all starts with finding our purpose in life. *Why* do we wake up every morning? What difference do we want to make in the world?

Most of us tend to dismiss this question of purpose at the onset, saying such concepts are for the rich and the privileged, while we are struggling just to make ends meet. We feel that we don't have the luxury of thinking beyond our everyday activities to address such a question. That is a very detrimental move. You don't need to be a master politician or a company's managing director to have a purpose. A purpose is not the reserve of the ones in power.

Each of us, from the humble intern to the most dynamic of CEOs, can and should have our life's purpose clear.

As the ancient Roman philosopher Seneca wrote, 'If a man knows not to which port he sails, no wind is favourable.'

While purpose gives us the direction in which to set sail and then helps us hustle to find favourable wind, not all pursuits can qualify as a purpose. As the famous author Cal Newport mentions, a well-defined purpose should consist of three essential elements:

1. *It has to matter to you*: Your purpose cannot be forced on you—it must be something that you find meaningful. Since you are unique, your purpose can be equally unique. It cannot be dictated by external elements like societal expectations or family pressure or even financial incentives. Your purpose is yours, your own, your precious!

2. *It has to be bigger than you*: A strong purpose is not a strategic move for personal gain or for the next promotion. It will not guide you to focus on your wealth, or success or status. Your purpose will gain significance, and you will be able to find long-term fuel within yourself only when you pursue an objective whose impact goes far beyond you. A feeling of awe is the true mark of getting close to defining your purpose.

3. *It needs to have a future orientation*: Finally, your purpose has to be forward-looking. Purpose does not focus on short-term gains or temporary satisfaction; it involves long-term commitment and growth. It should guide your decisions, actions and aspirations in the

long term. True purpose demands investments and sacrifices but rewards you with growth and sustained motivation.

With the alignment of these three elements, we arrive at our definition of purpose, which can be a powerful guiding force for our future decisions, inspiring resilience and bringing lasting satisfaction. But before finding what matters to you and what is bigger than you, you need to first answer: who are you?

You are a massive triumph of nature and are highly unique. As the eminent author Robert Greene espouses, billions of events had to happen for your particular DNA to be formed. You are unique because your DNA has never been formed earlier and will never do so again. You have infinite potential just because of who you are. Adding to this, the experiences that shape our lives are all unique to us. No one else in the world has had the same upbringing, same challenges, same opportunities and same experiences as you. You are one of a kind, and that uniqueness is your power.

The million-dollar question is, do you recognise who you are? Are you aware of your own true self? The upcoming sections will guide you to finding that deep-rooted seed of uniqueness and helping you understand who you are and who you want to be. Only after building this awareness and finding answers to these important questions can we hope to improve our relationship with time.

That is because, before wondering about where to find more time, a better question to answer is what to do with the time we *do* have. Whether it is leading nations or teaching the next generation, what is the purpose—big or small—of our existence? The answer will then guide us to make the necessary choices in our lives to find time for what matters, and use that time to the best of our ability.

- Achieving milestone after milestone cannot give us lasting happiness.
- Lasting happiness can never be acquired by running for a promotion, designation or an achievement. It is never found by 'becoming something'.
- Only a journey of purpose can give lasting happiness.
- Purpose has three elements:
    1. It has to matter to you;
    2. It has to be bigger than you;
    3. It needs to have a future orientation.
- The path to finding your purpose begins by first building an understanding of who you are.

CHAPTER 2

Finding Your Why

THE FIRST STEP TO FINDING OUR PURPOSE IS TO BE comfortable with asking ourselves uncomfortable questions. One of the biggest obstacles to this is the intimidation we feel just at the thought of it. The hypnotic and comfortable rhythms of our busy lives are easier than asking ourselves to pause, reflect and work to find ourselves. We might end up not liking what we discover.

Another problem is our mistaken belief that our purpose is immaterial unless it is grand, something that has the power to change the world! Some of us get lost in peer pressure and become engineers or finish MBAs without considering our next steps, and thus end up adrift, with no clear direction.

Clearly, these are not easy questions to answer. They make you uncomfortable. But those who take time and make some effort to answer the 'what' of their life have a greater chance of understanding the 'how' of it. Yet it is essential to avoid getting stuck in this. The 'what' is not a destination that one can reach; it is not a state of perfection; it is not even unchanging. The best we can do is hope to find a general direction where we want our ship to sail and keep checking that we are headed where we want to go. The quest to find our purpose is not at all like the Google Maps aunty directing us with door-to-door navigation along the shortest route. Finding your purpose and staying true to its course is more like wayfinding in ancient times, a ship at sea making its way along at night, with the North Star as the marker.

The first step towards finding your purpose is to go deep within yourself to figure out who you are. Let's try a few experiments and see if any of them helps us find an answer to this question. Note down your honest answers to the exercises below.

Exercise

Think of a deep-rooted experience. Go back to your childhood, replay some key moments and answer the questions below with a strong, connected rationale.

1. What is my unique strength? What is the seed of that strength?
2. What is my unique area of improvement? What is the seed of that weakness?

Go deep into your childhood and teenage years to find the answer. Think of your school days, your summer holidays, your old friends or your college buddies, and your interactions with them. Only by first understanding the seed of our strengths and weaknesses can we start building the foundations of our purpose.

I will explore my own strengths and origin story as an example.

Q. What's my unique strength and the seed of that strength?

From my interactions with colleagues and their feedback, I know that speed of execution and delivering results on time are among my key strengths. To find the source, I would go back to my early school days. Like all kids, I used to love playtime. But my parents had a strict rule: playtime privileges were activated only when I had finished all my homework. If I finished early, I could start playing early; if I procrastinated and didn't finish it on time, it would reduce my playtime. This rule gave me immense clarity, even as a child, that I had to finish my homework with passable quality and maximise my playtime. Execution with speed and passable quality was built into me as my go-to mode, which I have carried in my dealings with office work.

As soon as I set or receive a deadline, my inner clock starts ticking. I start planning, moving people along and running with the aim of getting that task out of my tray. This habit has led to me delivering most of my commitments on time.

Q. What's my unique area of improvement and the seed of that weakness?

The story about my homework-first-and-play-second upbringing has also, in my view, led to my biggest weakness.

In my endeavour to finish things on time and to always run towards deadlines, I have lost the art of patience. If

I get stuck on a complicated piece of work that takes me longer than I planned, it makes me impatient. I become cranky and irritable, and lose focus. My desire to go out and have a good time and my inability to do so because of this annoying, difficult task frustrates me.

As Franz Kafka says, there are two cardinal sins from which all others spring: impatience and laziness. My impatience brings out a bad side of me that I want to avoid. I have recently become aware of this and am trying to work on it.

This exercise should give us a good understanding of who we are. We can add further dimensions to it. Let's do another experiment.

The Three Me's

Virginia Woolf famously wrote, 'I am not one and simple, but complex and many.' I believe this is true for all of us. We are multiple people in one, interconnected yet different at different times. We love and care for people but are super aggressive at strangers when stuck in traffic. We are demanding and non-compromising at the workplace and yet completely surrender to the ones we love. We let our emotions flow when watching a particularly touching movie alone but build a wall if someone is watching alongside us, lest they think we are weak. We are not one; we are many. We are not simple; we are complex.

In my view, there are three broad personalities within us:

- *The Seed*: This is the most basic part of us. The seed is our ancestral brain: the amygdala and the hippocampus, where our most basic memories, our past, our upbringing and our core personality are stored. This is where resides our natural instinct that tells us fire is bad, snake is bad, pointy rock is bad—run. The seed is very powerful, but in our daily hustle, it lies mostly dormant, silently supporting our physical reflexes and allowing us to continue making more complex choices without much interference. It rears its head when we feel hunger pangs or primitive road rage.

- *The Lone Wolf*: This is the part of us that we only show ourselves, emerging when we are alone. This is our true identity. This is the tree that has grown from the seed and has taken full form with all its complexities and is in touch with the reality of life. This is the identity that comes to the fore when we dance like no one is watching. Those extremely lucky few who find understanding partners get to share this part of themselves. This is our true self, to each their own.

- *Dr Jekyll*: In the famous story by R.L. Stevenson, the reputed Dr Jekyll transforms into the despicable Mr Hyde to indulge in his dark desires. In my view, Hyde was the true personality, and Dr Jekyll the mask. We all transform into our own Dr Jekyll avatars too, showing our best face to the society. We hide our Hyde, our lone wolf, beneath the veneer of the sociable Dr Jekyll.

Exercise: The Three Me's

Take a sheet of paper and identify these three personalities within you. Reflect on your behaviours, think about your upbringing and childhood, the key moments that come to your mind, and write down the answers to the following questions:

The Seed

What values do you hold the closest to your heart? (Google the names of values; it will help you in creating a laundry list from which you can choose values that align with your Seed. For example, some of them are integrity, fairness, compassion, gratitude, humility, generosity, honesty.)

Values:____

The Wolf

What activities and behaviours do you exhibit when you are alone (apart from dancing or singing in the shower)? Think of the last few days and reflect on what you did, what you watched, what you listened to and what thoughts came to your mind when you were alone.

Emotions:____

Thoughts:____

Behaviours:____

The Jekyll

Think about the recent times when you had to fake it to make it, when you found yourself making an effort to conform to societal norms and expectations.

Situation:____

Why you needed to pretend:_________________________

How you pretended:________________________________

Emotions:____

Thoughts:____

If you have filled the exercises above with honest, hand-to-heart answers, you will have found some truths about your personality. Things that we already know about ourselves take on a whole new meaning when we see them in black and white.

Now that we have spent some time understanding our Seed, our Wolf, and our Jekyll, and have deep-dived into our unique strengths and areas of improvement, along with their origins, we are well-equipped to start the next part of the journey of finding our purpose.

- Ask yourself uncomfortable questions about your deeper self to start the journey to find your purpose.
  - Reflect on your childhood, your formative teenage years and answer two questions:
  - What is my unique strength? What is the seed of that strength?
  - What is my unique area of improvement? What is the seed of that weakness?
- We have three layers of self:
  - The Seed: Our deep-rooted, primal core that rarely comes to surface unless we feel strong emotions.
  - The Lone Wolf: Our true personality that we showcase just to ourselves, our uninhibited concept of who we are.
  - Dr Jekyll: The mask we wear to interact with people and blend into society.

CHAPTER 3

What Drives Us

THE EPIC MOVIE *CHAK DE INDIA*, THROUGH THE JOURNEY of Coach Kabir Khan and the Indian women's hockey team, beautifully illustrates the power of understanding what drives us and the impact it can create by aligning our drivers with a greater purpose.

When Kabir Khan first takes over as the coach, he brings with him his own ideals, rigid discipline, tough leadership and national pride. While his vision is clear, even noble, he fails to understand his team members' motivations. He expects them to blindly follow his idea of teamwork, discipline and sacrifice for the nation. However, he fails to realise that these ideals do not work for his team, which is fractured, driven by personal rivalries, state-based loyalties and buckling under everyone's lack of faith in their potential. His methods are a complete failure and the players plot to get him fired.

His breakthrough comes when he sees the team for who they are, when he stops imposing his ideals and understands theirs instead. He realises that these women are not just playing hockey but are fighting for respect— from their families, from society, from the world of male-dominated sports. Each player is facing her own personal battle. When he realises their true driver and understands that it is not just about the trophy but about proving their worth to a society that constantly undermines them, he is able to shape them into a formidable, champion team.

We need to be in touch with our deepest drivers to bring out the best in us. As kids, our requirement set is very limited. We are naturally motivated, curious and full of energy to try new things and perform to the best of our abilities. As we grow up, our identity becomes narrower, with strong preferences that develop over time. We start to see ourselves through the lenses of the subjects we take in college, the path we embark on with our first job, and so on. Eventually, due to circumstances, peer pressure or just pure coincidence, we arrive at a point where what the world pays us for isn't necessarily the activity that gives us the most satisfaction.

As we grow professionally, we might become proficient at *what* we do; with the experience we gain, we might know very well *how* to do it, but we might be completely unaware of *why* we are doing it. Especially on the bad days, you must be asking yourself: why am I in this job? Am I here just following the sheep—my friends and peers—and do I want to continue doing this? Do I even enjoy this? Is this something I see myself doing throughout my adult life?

Finding your drivers requires you to answer these questions. So let's work on some more experiments to begin answering them. As earlier, take a sheet of paper and a pencil and fill in your honest answers to the questions or prompts asked below.

Find What Matters

Go through your life from childhood until now and note the three most prominently happy memories. Describe them in the following detail; I have shared an example of one of my core memories to illustrate:

	Where are you?	Describe the scene and all that your senses feel
Context	Setting	I am at a picnic near a serene waterfall close to the small town where I spent my childhood. There's green grass all around me.
	View	The leaves are dripping with raindrops, the sky is dusky blue and the air is clear after the rain.
	Smell	There is a damp and earthy smell of leaves and rain.
	Sounds	I can hear the gurgling of the waterfall nearby.
	Touch	I am absentmindedly touching the blades of grass as I chat with my friends.
	Taste	I can taste the water from the rain.

	Who is with you?	Describe your company, and outline who you like and who you dislike. It is equally important to note what we don't like and avoid, to know what has shaped us.
People	Family	I am with my parents and sister. My sister is playing with my friends and me, and my parents are chatting with their friends.
	Friends	I am with some of my friends. I don't necessarily like all of them. One of them is particularly nasty to me, and I always try to avoid him. But I am hanging out with the people I like.
	Larger Group	I am part of a large group of my parents' friends who have come for a picnic. I have always enjoyed going on picnics with my family and a large group that makes me feel welcome and safe.

	What are you doing?	Describe what is happening. Use only verbs and adverbs to describe clear action statements. Describe what others in the scene are doing.
Actions	All	Family and friends are chatting with their feet dipped in a pool of water.
		Kids are playing below the waterfall and making a lot of noise.
		I feel the cool water of the waterfall flow by and am singing a song.
		We are all hungry and waiting for the lunch of dal bati, my favourite.

Emotions	What are you feeling?	Describe your state of mind. Go deep and give names to the various sensations and multitude of emotions you are experiencing.
	Happiness	Warmth at the company and the setting; such a beautiful place to be, such fantastic weather and fresh vibes.
	Gratitude	I am thankful for such a lovely day filled with fun and laughter with friends and family.
	Peace	I am content in the moment. I don't want anything further. No desire other than that this moment should continue and extend beyond its finiteness.
	Love	I feel loved, cared for and welcomed as part of the tribe.
	Relief	I am happy that the person I dislike is busy with another set of friends and that I don't have to play with him.
	Excitement	I am eagerly waiting to taste the sumptuous lunch that will follow shortly.

Take a piece of paper and list three core memories that stand out in as much detail as possible. (Scan the QR code to download the template for the table above.) All the memories don't need to be happy memories. You may list down a memory that visibly shakes you to the core, too, as it might have shaped you into the person you are today. What is essential is that it should stand out to you as a significant event in your lifetime, something that stirs you. When visually stitched together, these memories will give you some insights into what matters to you.

Find What Gives You Meaning

Let us now work on another experiment. Imagine a scenario where someone is writing your eulogy. This is not a family member, friend or work colleague, but someone who was impacted by your work, someone whose life was affected by how you lived your life and your contributions to society, someone whom you might have even inspired. What do you think they would write? Fill the following table.

Aspect	Reflection Prompts
Title (not more than 3–5 words)	____
Name and family	_________________________ was part of a loving family consisting of ___________ ____

Aspect	Reflection Prompts
Partner's thoughts	________________________, their partner, who is _________________________________ said about them: '________________________ _________________________________ _______________________________ '
Core values	They were best known for their values of _________________________________ and _____________________________________ which they lived by every day.
Achievements	Their greatest achievement was __________ _______________________________________, which they accomplished by _____________ ____
Impact on others	With this achievement, they had a positive impact on the lives of _________________ ____________________________, by bringing about change in the form of ____________ ____
Hobbies and passions	They were passionate about .____________ ____ ____
Strongest qualities	According to those who knew them best, their strongest quality was _____________ __________________________, which they displayed the most when __________________________ ____

Aspect	Reflection Prompts
Overcoming challenges	One of their defining moments was when they overcame __________________ __________________ by __________________ __________________
Professional journey	Professionally, they grew from __________ __________________ to __________ __________________ to __________ __________________, showing growth and perseverance over the years.
Leadership style	They were known for their leadership style, characterised by __________________ __________________, and they inspired their team by __________________ __________________
Relationships and connections	They were known for their deep connections with __________________ __________________, and they touched lives through their ability to __________________ __________________
Legacy and contributions	They left behind a legacy of __________ __________________, which continues to inspire __________________ __________________
Financial and material legacy	They have left an estate valued at approximately __________________ __________, including assets such as __________ __________________

Aspect	Reflection Prompts
Moral legacy	Their moral legacy includes teachings such as ___________________ ___________________ ___________________, which will guide future generations.
How they will be remembered	They will be remembered most for their __ ___________________ ___________________
Final reflections	In the end, their life was a testament to ___ ___________________ They lived with a purpose of ___________ ___________________ ___________________

This exercise gives us a visual and firm reminder of what matters the most to us, what our ultimate desire is today. Desires are transient; with new information and experiences, they will change. But as of today, this is the kind of eulogy we would want to live for. This North Star should help us take future decisions that align with it and steps that help us continue moving towards reaching it. Armed with this, let us now bring things a bit closer home.

If the eulogy experiment is a good way to shake you and make you reassess what is important in life, the next experiment designed by authors Bill Burnett and Dave Evans in their book *Design Your Life* brings the perspective closer home. I have made some personal additions to this system to tweak it to my needs.

Answer the following questions with a horizon of no more than three years in mind. Also, for questions about how many hours we have to spare in a week, let us do some quick maths. If we sleep about eight hours a day, then in a week, we have

$$\text{Total Hours in a week} - \text{hours spent sleeping}$$
$$= 24 \times 7 - 8 \times 7 = 112$$

The sum total of the hours you mention for each year, in the shaded black rows, should not exceed 112.

Think about your life and the path you are on. Where will you be three years from now? Put in the dimensions below for each upcoming year for the next three years. Year 1 is what your reality of today is. Year 2 is where you want to go, what changes you want to bring in your life in the coming one year. Even if you don't completely revamp your life, what are the incremental changes you would want to bring in? You will be spending your 112 hours in a particular pattern now, in the first year. Do you want to bring a change to this 112-hour distribution in the next year? Do you want to give more time to family or to your hobbies or to your own learning? Where should you reallocate the time from? Which activity can you cut back on so you can reallocate that time to something else you want to do? Assuming you are living a typical day today, how should your typical day in the future look?

Refer to the eulogy above while filling out the Odyssey Plan to know that you are heading in the broad direction you want your life to take and that your wayfinding is on point.

The Odyssey Plan

	A Day in Life	Year 1 (Reality today)	Year 2 (Your life next year)	Year 3 (Your life in two years)
1	Wake-up routine			
Commute to and from work				
2	What key project are you working on?			
3	At what time do you return home? What do you do after you return?			
4	When do you go to sleep? What is your total sleep time?			

Relationships and love				
5	Are you in a relationship? On a scale of 1–10, how strong is your bond?			
6	How much undivided attention and time in hours in a week do you give to the relationship?			
Family				
7	How many members are present in your immediate family? Of these members, who all live with you?			

8	How much undivided attention and time in hours in a week do you give to the family?			
Friends				
9	How many deep friendships do you have?			
10	How much undivided attention and time in hours in a week do you give to your friends?			
Personal passion				
11	Do you have any hobbies, interests or personal projects that you are consistently working on?			

12	How much undivided attention and time in hours in a week do you give to your personal passions?			
13	How proficient are you in these personal passions—novice, beginner, amateur, professional, virtuoso?			
Work and career growth				
14	What role are you in? What's your designation?			
15	What skills are you proficient at?			

16	How many hours in a week do you spend working on your current role?			
Money growth				
17	What is your monthly take-home salary? How much of that do you save / spend?			
18	What is your bank balance and investment portfolio?			
19	On a scale of 1–10, how comfortable are you with the estate of money that you have?			

Learning plan				
20	To reach the next year's role growth, what is the most important new skill that you need to pick up?			
21	How are you learning this skill? On the job/ mentorship/ course/ training?			
22	How many hours in a week do you spend learning this new skill?			
Health and body				
23	On a scale of 1–10, how will you rate your health? What is your BMI?			

24	How many hours of exercise and other health-improving activities per week are you putting in?			
Mind				
25	How stressed do you feel on a scale of 1–10?			
26	What causes this stress for you?			
27	What destresses you, how do you destress?			
28	How many hours in a week do you spend on this destressing activity?			

Soul				
29	On a scale of 1–10, how much emotional baggage do you carry? On a scale of 1–10, how much effort do you make to unload this emotional baggage?			
30	What steps are you taking to be emotionally healthy to enrich your soul?			
31	How many hours in a week are you spending on this soul-enriching activity?			

The more truthfully and honestly you do this fairly intense exercise, the more insight you will gain to what matters to you, where you think you are and where you want to go in the near future.

Exercise: Let's Shake Things Up

Make a new table, a new plan, with one key difference. (Use the template you can download from the QR code below.) Assume you have a fallout with your current company, and you cannot work there again. You cannot even work in the same function again. If you are a doctor, you cannot be a doctor again. You are forced to choose an alternative path. Write down what that path would be and the answers for all the questions in the same table.

Now comes the most radical shake-up of all. Ignore whatever you have written in the past two tables and draw up a third table. Remove the constraints of money, society, expectations, etc. If you do not have to answer to anyone else in life for the next three years, be it your parents, nosy uncles, your friends or what people will think and you have all the money in the world, what will your next three years look like? Chart out that radical path for yourself, keeping in mind the eulogy to guide you.

These three versions help us get a good understanding of where we think we are, where we think we are going, what alternatives or options we think we can explore and, most importantly, what is holding us back. Once we are clear about this information, starting now, we will be able to make more informed decisions about our lives and keep guiding them towards our purpose.

Let's now shorten the timeline: what should our upcoming year look like? What should our priorities be for the coming year? There are a few fun exercises to arrive at that.

Happy Birthday!

Imagine you are celebrating your birthday next year. You have a nice party at your place with friends and family—excellent music, hearty food and good vibes. Suddenly, someone clinks a glass and asks you three things you are thankful for: changes, improvements or achievements you are proud of in the past year. What would be those three things that have brought you closer to your North Star? In the table below, write one achievement/improvement for each. I have given a random example to illustrate each.

Dimension	Connections	Improvement/ Change / Achievement	Your turn
Relationships	Love, family, friends	I took my parents on a five-day trip to Dubai.	

| Work | Career growth, money growth, skill learning | I got a new role as the head of operations for a new company and learnt a new programming language. | |
| Being | Mind, body, soul, health | I practised pranayama daily for ten minutes and achieved my target BMI | |

This exercise is a fun experiment to bring to life the tacit thoughts of self-improvement, changes for the betterment of self that are hovering just below the surface of your conscience. With a timeline of one year, you might be able to find this more relatable and achievable, and can start planning for the same.

Exercise: Wheel of Life

We can use the broad sections from the exercises above to do another impactful exercise. For this, we envision our life as a wheel, a circle of all our multitude of experiences, relationships, work and desires.

In the space below, divide the wheel into some broad dimensions of life. You may add or delete any dimension that matters to you. I have used some of the same dimensions as in the Odyssey Plan exercise above.

Divide the wheel into four quarters. The first quarter represents your relationships, the second quarter your work, the third quarter your 'self'—your physical, mental and spiritual health—and the fourth quarter represents your will, your agency through which you interact with the world. Now divide each quarter into three parts, as shown in the image.

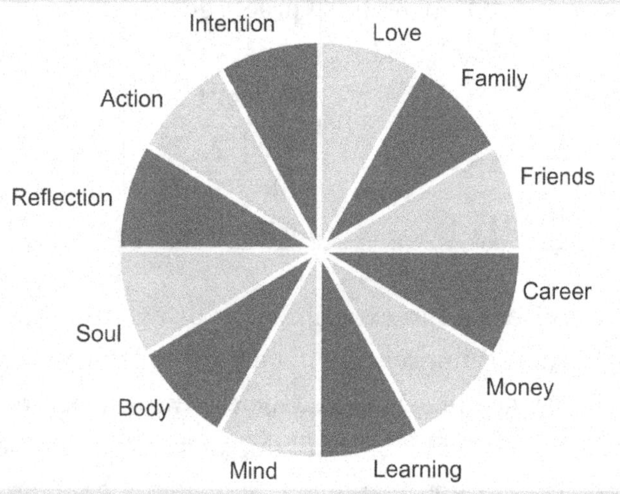

Understanding Will

While the sections on relationships, work and self are easy to understand, let us explore the concept of will. Your will is your agency, the driving force behind your interactions between your being and your environment. One of the first steps needed to get control on the puzzle of time is to develop an awareness of your will, about your interactions with your environment and then act on improving those interactions. Will has three dimensions:

1. *Reflection* addresses how deeply we go inwards to process the information we receive from our environment. How much do we reflect on our past, present and future? What is the quality of that reflection? Do we brood and sulk? Or do we observe the events with a detached and forgiving lens, and determine what needs to change to drive the world towards our wants and needs? Reflection is the starting point for any positive change in life.

2. *Action* here indicates deliberate action. Are you a positive change agent in your life, or are you letting things happen to you? We are all at different life stages and might have different levels of control over our day. People just starting their careers might have little choice in how they want to spend their day, but even an intern can choose to take deliberate, honest action on the tasks assigned to them. Reflect on how much of your day is spent taking deliberate actions.

3. *Intention* is the ultimate level of will and freedom. Because what is freedom, if not the power and ability to spend time doing what one intends? If you reflect upon what you want to change and then spend your time on relevant activities with deliberate action, you are truly free. To improve our relationship with time, intention is the key. Doom scrolling on social media is spending time without intention. Well-formed intention based on solid reflection and performed by deliberate action is the trifecta of will, and only when we will, we can.

Filling in the Wheel

With this understanding of the four sections, let us rate ourselves on this wheel of life.

The first principle of rating here should be the alignment with our eulogy goals. Rate yourself on each of these dimensions on how close to your eulogy goals you are for this year. Don't be strict and unforgiving—this wheel is not to be publicised; it is your personal life audit. Be honest yet forgiving.

Rate yourself with 10 as the best role model, ideal of that particular dimension that comes to your mind. For the love section, let 10 be a love as sincere and deep as Raj and Simran from *Dilwale Dulhania Le Jayenge*, and 1 can be the loneliness that Anjali felt seeing Rahul choose Tina in *Kuch Kuch Hota Hai*. For family, you may look to Barjatyas and their magnum opus *Hum Saath – Saath Hain* for deep family ties, and 1 can be the horrors of *Baghban*. All of us lie somewhere in between these extremes.

Work

For the section about work, think about where you are and where you would have wanted to be today. Don't compare yourself with the CEO. A CEO or a senior leader can most certainly be a role model and aspiration, but we all have different journeys. Hence, don't set the bar of aspiration so high that you get intimidated and give up. Assess your career: has it grown at a 10, with consistent role enhancements, awards, rewards and recognition? Or is it at 1—routine, thankless, mundane, a job that you want to run away from.

For money growth, have you comfortably reached where you wanted to be from a financial security standpoint? Or is there a long way to go? It is not necessary to be rich like Scrooge McDuck and swim in our personal coin bank to rate ourselves a 10. It should work well if we are on our way to our financial goal and can sleep peacefully at night.

The currency of learning is skills. Reflect on whether you have added any valuable skills recently that will propel you to perform better at work. If you have learned three or four new skills with decent proficiency, be generous and rate yourself well. If multiple skills still need to be learnt to reach your aspirations within the year, rate yourself a bit lower accordingly.

Will

Consider your few average days in recent months for the section on will. If you were undertaking positive reflection and giving some minimum quality time to reflect and correct the course, rate yourself higher. If you have never stopped to reflect, are jumping from one task to the other, juggling multiple priorities and can barely catch your breath, rate yourself much lower.

Action

For action, as translated for knowledge workers, if you took planned and deliberate steps to finish some deliveries, rate yourself well. If you delivered well, planned strategies and executed them well, rate yourself highly. Rate yourself low if you were running on the rat wheel, not acting with your total energy and interest. For intention, if you spend time only in the way you planned to or intended to, rate yourself high. If you are left wondering where time vanishes and have no memory of the last few days and what you did with them, rate yourself lower.

Fill in the wheel with a pencil to correspond with your rating, and voila, you instantly have a visual recap of your life and where you are. Below is a wheel I made at the start of this financial year.

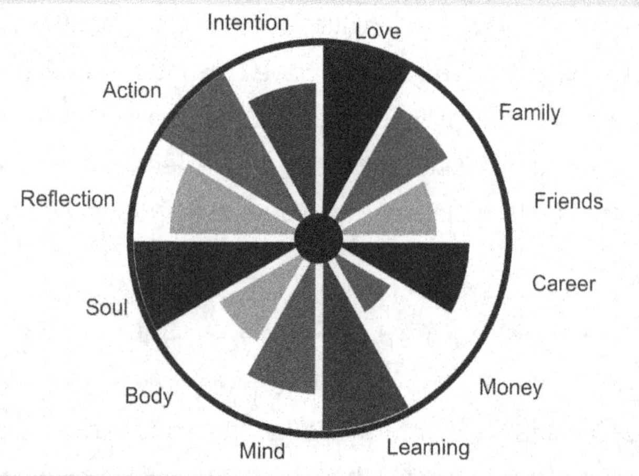

Now, looking at the wheel, we need to reflect and take a call on the top actions we want to take over the upcoming year to change the shading in any dimension. An unbalanced wheel is representative of some dimensions being neglected. Who wants a bumpy ride in an unbalanced and oddly shaped wheel?

It is important to note that in one year, we won't be able to radically go from a 5 to a 10. We must decide what incremental change we want to make and what it translates to. For example, given my sedentary lifestyle, I have been severely neglecting my health . Hence the low rating. But I am now thinking of making a change and would want to make the shift from a rating of 2—where my sugar levels are haywire, my energy levels are low and my exercise hours are near zero—to a rating of 4, which, for me, translates to some simple incremental changes. I plan to do thirty minutes of exercise and pranayama in the morning and walk 8,000 steps daily for five days a week. This should bring my sugar levels under control. This looks like a manageable and trackable goal and doesn't intimidate me. I have not suddenly thought of going to a 10 and desiring a chiseled body like Salman or Hrithik or even becoming a marathon runner over a year. Focus on the next bite-sized step that you are not afraid to take.

This is a fun yet impactful exercise and an experiment we can run every quarter. Why don't you take your phone out and put a calendar entry for the first Sunday of every quarter? This will remind you to make your wheel of life at the start of every quarter, and track your progress over the year.

In this section, we have explored the reasons for even bothering to read this book. Why do we need time? What do we want to do with our time? What difference will it make if we get more or less time? We have decoded our own selves, and these experiments have helped our ship find our North Star, our purpose.

Now, let us look at what drives this ship ahead. Before we deep-dive into concepts on how to grab more time and what to do with it, let us first understand what fuels us to do anything at all, to journey through the passage of time. Before we know the clock of time, let us understand what makes our clock tick.

- The first step to finding our purpose is to go deep down memory lane and complete the Bright Memory exercise.
- Write your eulogy to know what gives your life meaning.
- To bring clarity on purpose in the near term, work on the Odyssey Plan and plot your life over the next three years.
- Imagine your next birthday and point out what achievements you will include in your speech.
- Plot your life's most important dimensions—relationships, work, health and will—on the Wheel of Life. Visually understand where the wheel is imbalanced and needs work.

CHAPTER 4

The Secret of Our Energy

JUST RECENTLY, AT AN OFFICE EVENT CALLED 'BRING Your Kids to Work Day', I witnessed a few five- to seven-year-olds wreck the otherwise monotonous office routine. They were running all around, jumping on desks and pushing each other; Post-Its were flying out, pens were finding bins and kids were yelling at their parents, squirming out of their reach. All this, at 6 p.m., when most of the employees are so tired after a heavy workday that they usually find themselves dreaming about home and what they will watch tonight on Netflix.

But something strange was happening as these kids rampaged through the office. There was a sudden increase in the buzz across the cubicles. People who were slumped at their laptops just a little while back were now found crackling with excitement, some with positive glee. When I asked what was going on, one of my colleagues mentioned that the kids brought in 'mad levels of energy' and that everyone was feeding off this liveliness in the workspace.

I am sure all of us have experienced this in our lives. Cute little puppies, electrifying music, our favourite dessert, a sport we love and sometimes just an interaction with some people leave us feeling fully charged, invigorated. Other things drain us, make us feel like we have no energy at all. We have often used these sentences at work: 'I just don't have the energy to deal with this' or 'I am so charged right now that I can finish my monthly targets today itself'. This ebb and flow of energy occurs across our life, depending on the situation we are in.

We have all also experienced how our energy fluctuates throughout the day. Morning people are bursting with energy as the day begins, and during the day, depending on how their day goes, their battery powers up or down. Some of us hate early mornings but are completely fine to party till the wee hours. But have you noticed that the energy you have when playing a competitive sport, let's say a challenging round of badminton, is of a different kind when compared to the energy you have when you are jogging through a park or partying late with friends?

Borrowing from the concept of yin and yang, I believe these different kinds of energies are basically just two types in various proportions. I call them Bright Energy and Dark Energy. Let us deep-dive into what these are and how they affect us. Once we understand the human energy system and the source of our power, we will see it as an essential ingredient to improving our relationship with time.

The Human Energy System

We all love our phones, are obsessed with them, are addicted to them and can't live without them, and our phone battery dying is our worst nightmare. This is because our phone anchors us and connects us to the world. We are remotely connected to our parents, friends, well-wishers, cab drivers and all kinds of distractions that keep us occupied via the tiny devices in our hands.

But, at the same time, we are blissfully unaware of our own battery system. What powers us, what drives us and what, at times, stops us?

Drawn here is a simple diagram of a circuit for the standard torch. There are two batteries connected by a switch to the bulb. When the switch is off, as in Diagram 1, the power doesn't flow in the circuit, and the bulb doesn't light up. In Diagram 2, the power flows in the circuit when the switch is on or connected and the bulb lights up. This simple principle is how all our electrical and electronic devices power up. Typically, torches use two batteries, and their electrical circuit will look like Diagram 3.

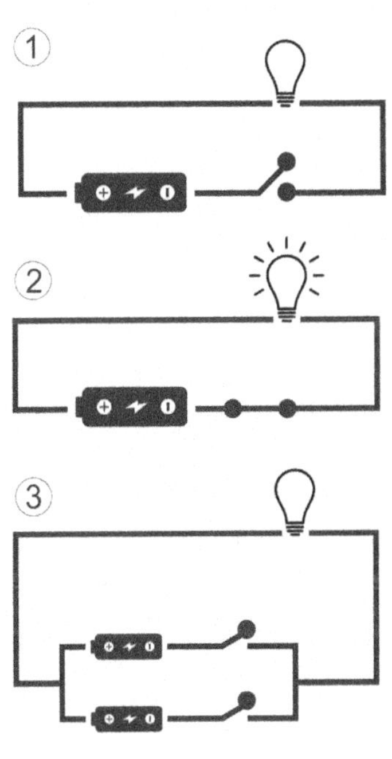

Now, let us add some complexity to this example. Like our laptop and mobile screens, some torches have the option to adjust to varying brightness levels. Now, this book is not a refresher course on electrical engineering; hence, we will not deep-dive into how (resistance, inductance, etc.), we can vary the brightness by controlling the power flow from the two batteries. So, a simple diagram of a system with brightness intensity control looks like this—Diagram 4. A power flow controller controls how much power goes through from each battery. It can stop all power from the first battery and let only the second battery power the bulb and vice versa. Hope you are with me.

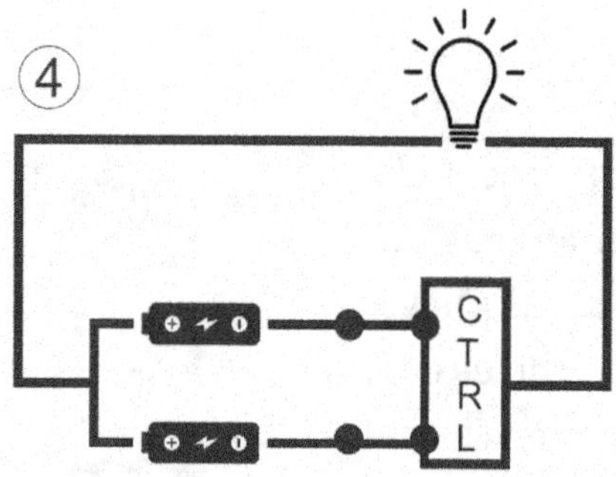

Now, let us translate this system to our human selves. Without bringing alive memories of the movie *The Matrix*, let us replace the circuit in the previous experiment with our whole selves, our mind, body and soul, as in Diagram 5. This human system is powered by our soul, which is deep within us, running on two sources of power (batteries): Bright Energy and Dark Energy. Our mind, the brain (controller), controls these energy sources and decides how much and what kind of energy goes through the system to the body, our being and our physical manifestation (bulb).

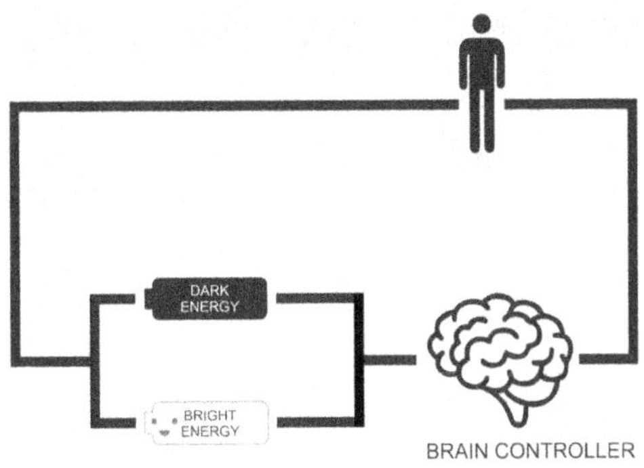

Let us add the final element to this human system. The circle around the body in Diagram 6 is the environment with which we interact. It includes both physical and emotional, tangible and intangible aspects, ranging from our home to our office, a beach in Goa to the nature trails of Mussoorie, friends we hang out with to the frenemy we dislike, Netflix shows we binge on to the boring meetings we attend.

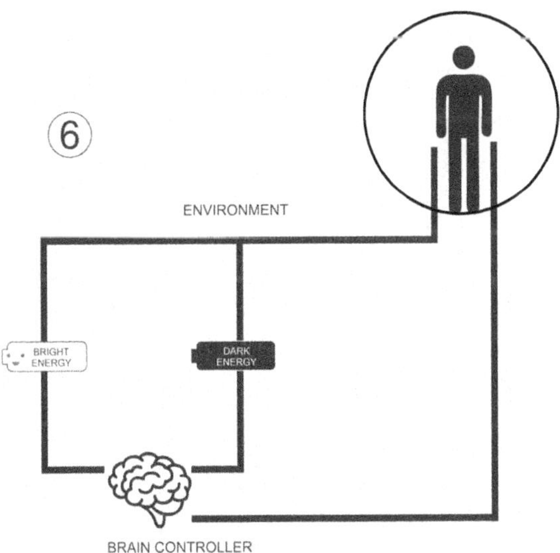

This system is complete in itself. The two batteries of Bright and Dark Energy, controlled by the mind, power us through the waking hours and enable us to interact with the environment and take in various experiences. These batteries, in turn, get recharged or depleted depending on these interactions and experiences with the environment. Once we sleep, the entire system goes into recuperation mode, and these batteries get a chance to be recharged naturally.

Why Two Energies?

Why do we even need these two energies? Why can we not be powered by just one source? Both energies have their respective importance. As the name suggests, Bright Energy is the source of all things good and positive. It gives us hope, happiness, drive, warmth and the fuel to go out into the world and do great deeds. The Bright Energy battery charge goes up when we pass it on to others through our positive words or actions. It also increases when we brighten somebody else's day through our support or even a simple smile. Bright Energy is the source of all things humane, of humanity itself.

Why, then, do you think we need another battery for Dark Energy? Let us go back and think about our ancestors. Living in caves, in small tribes, life for the cave dweller would have been hard. To complicate things further, there were dangerous predators all around. If we had only Bright Energy, we wouldn't have been able to develop the instinct to differentiate between what is good for us and what is bad. Dark Energy is the power that helps us learn to fear certain necessary things and builds our intuitive response to things we need to run away from. Fire bad, run. Big cat bad, run. Even in today's modern context, Dark Energy comes to our rescue multiple times daily. Dark Energy drives our response to danger, our aggression when we perceive a threat and our ability to understand risks. If Bright Energy is the source of humanity, Dark Energy is the basis of survival.

These two energies have many similarities in the way they operate. The first is their origin. Both sprout from deep within our souls. The gush of immense happiness on holding one's own baby and the deep fear experienced when walking down an unsafe street in some of our cities have the same source, the same seed: the energy core. This core interacts with the human body through the controller of the mind. More on the controller and these interactions later.

The second similarity is that they grow in contact with similar energies. Our experiences and all things in the world can be divided into two depending on how they influence our internal energies.

1. *Bright Matter*: Things, people and activities that brighten your day, such as a smile, a walk in the park, meeting your friends and spending time with your family, are all feeding and growing each other's Bright Energy. The more you share, the more you feel the day brighten.

2. *Dark Matter*: Things, people and activities that darken your thoughts, let's call them Dark Matter, such as gloomy weather, bad company, unhealthy habits,

terrible bosses, toxic workplace and dangerous relatives, all feed an increase in Dark Energy, leading to a spiral of darkness and negativity.

One key difference between the two energies is their allure. Even though Bright Energy makes us happy and energetic, the default attraction of the human mind is towards Dark Energy. It may be because of our hunter–gatherer origin, where survival was the main goal, and spreading cheer would have taken a back seat. Seeking comfort and safety is our default setting because of the way we are wired. Sometimes, we like nothing more than doing nothing, being lazy and even feeling guilty after spending the entire day in front of the TV; passively letting the weekend go by is not strong enough to push us to action. To harness Bright Energy, we must make conscious efforts and be intentional about what we want to do. On the other hand, Dark Energy is our default state, and we love returning to it because it takes zero effort from our body.

Awareness is the first step in learning to harness these energies better. We need to acknowledge that we have both energies within us and that there will be times when one will dominate the other. Since we are no longer in mortal danger of being eaten by big cats in the jungle, for knowledge workers, it makes a lot more sense to over-index the usage of Bright Energy. The more we can bring our inner Bright Energy to the fore, the better the chances of happiness and higher the productivity. First, let's become aware of our energy core; second, let's understand what drives and controls our Bright and Dark Energies; and third, let's come up with a toolkit to harness your Bright Energy better, to understand your natural rhythms concerning your time. The goal is to help you to harness Bright Energy more often during the day, and lead high-quality lives.

Understanding our body's Bright and Dark Energy systems is a critical step in understanding and having time, improving our relationship with it and doing our best with the time we have. To manage time, we need to learn to manage energy first.

The Energy Audit

Before diving deep into harnessing Bright Energy, let us first understand our relationship with the two energy sources. How do we feel when Bright Energy forces are at play? And what is the impact of Dark Energy on our being?

Exercise: Bright Energy Audit

Note down your thoughts on the following checklist.

In the recent past, think of a day at work and the specific activity you did when you were your happiest. Be careful not to think about an outcome like a recent promotion or an award you won. The focus should be on an activity that would have made this outcome possible.

Write down a brief about three such activities in not more than 30 words in the space below. Do not exceed the space provided—brevity does wonders to crystalise an idea:

Bright Work Activity Details	Activity 1	Activity 2	Activity 3
Time on the clock when the activity was done			
Duration of the activity			
Specific nature of activity: for example, study, research, giving or receiving lecture, leading a meeting, giving a presentation			

Your key takeaway from the activity. Why did you feel happy?

Activity 1____

Activity 2____

Activity 3____

Now, think of three non-work activities where you felt happy and fulfilled. It can be anything close to your heart—something as simple as watching TV with your partner or as rigorous as cleaning the nearby river, or a good and intense workout session. Think of three such deeply personal activities and note down their details in the format below.

Bright Non-Work Activity Details	Activity 1	Activity 2	Activity 3
Time on the clock when the activity was done			
Duration of the activity			
Specific nature of activity: for example, practising a hobby, meeting friends, spending time with family, playing with your pet, jogging, working out.			

Your key takeaway from the activity. Why did you feel happy?

Activity 1____

Activity 2____

Activity 3____

From the exercise above, you should be able to derive some clarity on the following questions:

1. What makes you happiest?
2. What is the most important to you?
3. What time of the day do you feel happiest?
4. How long does it take for you to feel energetic enough to do any activity?

Your answers to these questions will give you some understanding of the Bright Energy within you and your relation with it. When noting the activities above, I am sure you would have felt a warm glow within you, a smile would have crossed your face and you would have felt your surroundings brighten. Even thinking about things that make us happy harnesses our Bright Energy.

Here we come to the crux of the matter: when you master your Bright and Dark Energies, you master your relationship with time, as you can use your time more intentionally to do things that increase your brightness.

Yet it is not only our likes but also our dislikes that shape us and our views of the world around us. Human beings are a collection of experiences, both good and bad. While it is important to know what brings out the Bright Energy in us, it is equally necessary to spend some time understanding what makes our Dark Energy battery roar. This awareness will tell us where and when our energy reserves go low, and how to take conscious steps to refuel.

Exercise: Dark Energy Audit

Let us repeat the energy audit, but we need to understand our Dark Energy moments this time.

Think of a standard work day and record when you feel low. This feeling need not be because of getting strong or negative feedback on a recent work submission. Think of moments when you just didn't want to physically be present in the workspace, when you felt an immediate need to take a break.

Think of a time when you felt sleepy and disinterested in the work. A time when you felt your energy battery go kaput and wanted a strong shot of caffeine. Think of three such moments/activities and record them in the tables below.

Dark Work Activity Details	Activity 1	Activity 2	Activity 3
Time on the clock when you felt low			
Duration of the activity			
Specific nature of activity: for example, routine work, back-to-back long meetings, meeting that could have been an email, boss's lecture, toxic teammates, etc.			

Your key takeaway from the activity. Why did you feel low on energy?

Activity 1____

Activity 2____

Activity 3____

From the exercise above, you should be able to derive some clarity on the following pieces:

1.   What takes away the brightness of your day?

2.   What aspects of your work don't matter to you?

3.   What time of the day do you feel your energy drop?

4.   When you start feeling the need for a break?

Only through awareness can we start work on harnessing these energies through intention. You should deep-dive further and do this exercise on a separate sheet of paper for as many Bright and Dark Energy activities as possible to understand what makes your day bright and not. Doing this step with as much detail as possible is crucial to decode our relationship with time.

Our daily activities can be divided into two broad buckets that we can call Energy Drivers. These Energy Drivers are of two kinds: Energy Brighteners and Energy Darkeners. Fill in the table below to chart out various activities you do during a typical day. Do they brighten your day or darken it?

Energy Brighteners	Energy Darkeners

The Activity Brightness (AB) Matrix

The intensity of Bright and Dark Energy release will vary for different activities. The Activity Brightness (AB) matrix is an excellent field to plot the various Brighteners and Darkeners we recorded above, along with the intensity of effect they have on our energy system. The point to note is that an increase in the intensity of Bright Energy doesn't necessarily mean that we will be jumping up and down. A quiet romantic date or a even simple dinner with your loved ones can increase our Bright Energy without any physical outburst. In the diagram below, I have plotted my Energy Drivers, and I strongly recommend that you plot your own Brighteners and Darkeners.

We can divide the activities into four quadrants as below:

- The Yellow Activities: high in activity energy and high in brightness
- The Green Activities: low in activity energy but high in brightness
- The Blue Activities: low in activity energy and low in brightness
- The Red Activities: high in activity energy but low in brightness.

Once you have plotted your activities in these four quadrants, reflect how your time is split between them. What percentage of your day is spent doing which kind of activities? Is this how you want to live? These are choices that become apparent to you when you see the colour map of your life visually through the AB matrix.

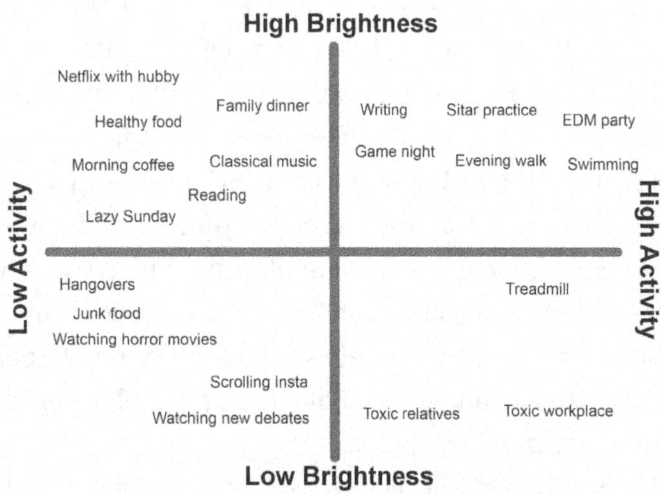

Bright Exercise: Activity Brightness Matrix

Plot your own AB Matrix after first noting down your Brighteners and Darkeners in the table above.

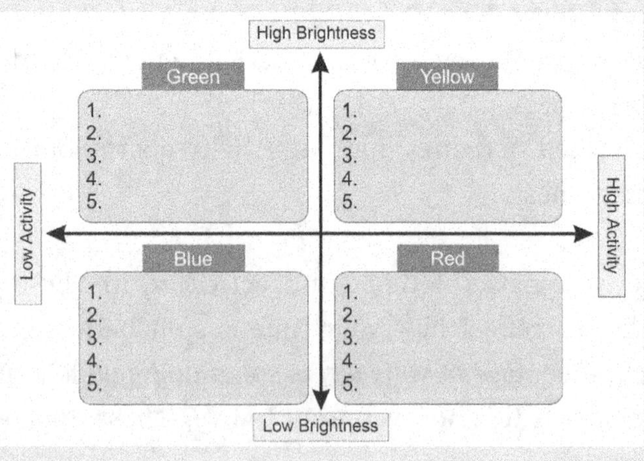

Along with these varying activity levels, the intensity of our Bright and Dark Energy fluctuates through the day. Understanding this ebb and flow of energy will help us tap into our reserves and eventually lead us to better time management.

Let us create a graph where you imagine your work day and give yourself a score ranging from +5 to -5. Zero is the basic energy that you start your day with. Positive 5 is the Bright Energy you feel at your happiest, most energetic self. Benchmark it with the Bright Energy you would have felt winning a recent competition, a complex challenge you overcame at work or the intense warmth and contentment you might have experienced on a great date.

Negative 5 is the feeling of gloom and darkness after a particularly shaking horror or post-apocalyptic movie, when you saw Snape kill Dumbledore and the sharp pinch of receiving a particularly sarcastic taunt from a toxic boss.

In the diagram below, I have showcased my energy flow on a typical day. Putting this graph to paper gave me many insights into how I spend my day. It helped me realise what doesn't work for me and what my energy flow looks like.

Note how my commute to and from the office brings out my Dark Energy as a result of my annoyance at the heat, traffic and boredom. Also, note how I am the most energetic during pre-lunch and pre-day closure hours. Understanding your energy rhythm is the first step to knowing your relationship with time and improving it.

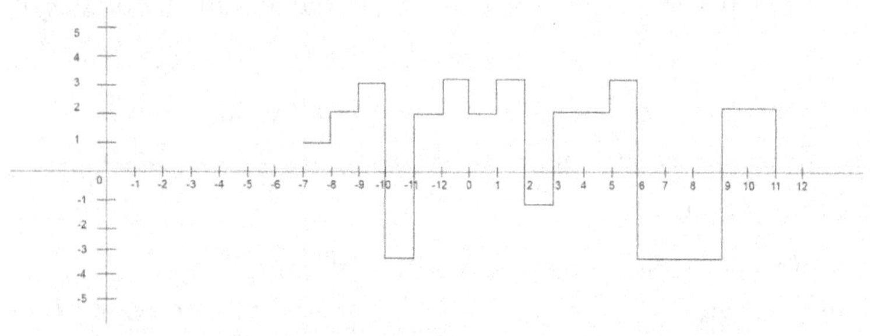

Exercise: Energy Flow Graph

Now chart your own daily energy in the space provided below.

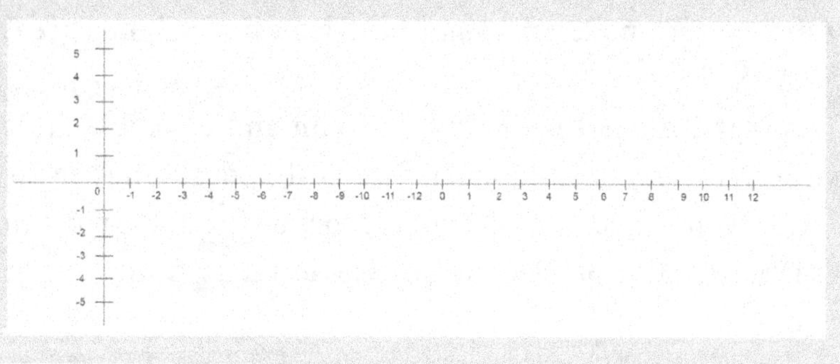

Armed with these details about our energy rhythm, our human energy system, the dual energy core and its interaction with the system, let us now look at how to create more and more moments during the day where Bright Energy dominates, leaving you happy, content and consciously intentional with the way you spend your time.

- The human energy system consists of two batteries: Bright Energy and Dark Energy.
- Bright Energy is the source of all things good and positive, giving us hope, happiness, drive and the fuel to go out into the world and do great deeds.
- Dark Energy drives our response to danger and our ability to calculate risks.
- Bright Energy is the source of humanity and Dark Energy is the basis of survival.
- Our mind is the controller that regulates the production, recharge and release of these two energies in our body.
- Our experiences and all things in the world can be divided into two depending on how they influence our internal energies:
  - Bright Matter: Things, people and activities that brighten our day;
  - Dark Matter: Things, people and activities that darken our thoughts.
- As our mind is designed to conserve energy and ensure survival, the default state of our body is to harness Dark Energy to keep us in comfort.
- To manage our time better, we need to learn to manage these energies first.
- We can divide all the activities we perform during the day into the Activity–Brightness (AB matrix) as below:

- The Yellow Activities: high in activity energy and high in brightness
- The Green Activities: low in activity energy but high in brightness
- The Blue Activities: low in activity energy and low in brightness
- The Red Activities: high in activity energy but low in brightness.

Section 2

Decoding Time

Chapter 5

Indian Standard Time

INDIANS HAVE A VERY COMPLICATED RELATIONSHIP WITH time. We are rarely on it. Be it the slumbering small towns of rural India or the bustling metropolis of Mumbai or Delhi, we always complain of having no time to explain our perpetual lateness. A casual attitude towards time seems to be deeply ingrained in our culture. Remember, all our home clocks used to be some minutes ahead on purpose. We have grown up always discounting five to ten minutes of whatever the clock is showing. One might even say we take comfort in mentally calculating the correct time by making clock adjustments rather than knowing the exact time. The clock shows 8 a.m., so don't worry; there are still five minutes, as the clock is ahead. It gives us a false sense of having more time.

As a culture, we are more collectivist than individualist. For us, the group is always bigger than the individual. Community and family take precedence over an individual. When coordinating large numbers of people in the community, with their different priorities, rigidity with timelines doesn't work. Deadlines must be flexible, and adjusting to other people's time must be allowed. One may even say that Indian time is event-oriented and not necessarily clock-oriented. We are more focused on ensuring the event for which time has been blocked takes place smoothly rather than fussing too much about whether it began or ended at the predetermined time. We don't like the certainty and finality that being on time and matching the rhythms to a clock gives, preferring to let things happen at their own pace. Adjusting expectations to a super consciousness of an abstract time horizon gives a broader error margin than a ruthless clock.

For us, being fashionably late to events is considered normal, even expected. If you arrive at the party venue at the time mentioned on the invite, you might find people roaming around in their pajamas, preparing for the party that will actually start at least an hour later. If we want guests to arrive at 8 p.m., our invite will say 7 p.m., knowing the first guest will come only after 7:30 or 8. This wide margin of error won't be possible if our society starts sticking to being punctual. It will take away the notional extra thirty to sixty minutes from organisers and the invitees, a loss we just cannot accept. This loss aversion of the notional extra time to do things drives all our behaviors.

In his seminal book *Four Thousand Weeks*, Daniel Burkeman says that time, unlike money, is a network good. He means that time has value only as a shared resource of the people within a network. One person coming on time won't make any difference to society's rhythms because everyone else is not following the same one.

Life in the cities adds multiple complications to this already strained relationship. Millions of people need to travel long distances every day from their homes to offices and back. A study by the Asian Development Bank on Mumbai's suburban rail network highlighted some interesting data.[1] Every day, 7.5 million passengers travel on Mumbai's 400-kilometre-long suburban railway network. Everyone is always in a mad rush. People who travel by road in cars or buses have it even worse. People in Mumbai can finish watching the entire series of *Friends* and *Modern Family* combined for the time they are stuck in traffic on average in a year. People in Bangalore have it far worse. Bangalore traffic jams are so hurtful that, as per a report from *Business Today*, the city loses US $25 billion in GDP just because people are stuck on the roads listening to RJs going on about traffic problems.[2] With this long and arduous commute, the quality of life in cities is taking a definite nosedive. The number of hours in a day starts counting for less, and everyone feels that they are constantly running with no end in sight. This daily routine leads to an overall decrease in Bright Energy and a corresponding increase in Dark Energy in our lives.

Add to this the work norms in Indian offices. We strongly subscribe to the old-school idea of 'seeing is believing'—if a

---

1   Sharad Saxena, 'Moving Millions with the Mumbai Metro', *ADB*, September 2019, https://www.adb.org/publications/moving-millions-mumbai-metro.

2   'Bengaluru's Economy Suffering Huge Loss of Rs 20,000 crore Anually due to Traffic Congestion, reveals study', *Business Today*, 7 August 2023, https://www.businesstoday.in/latest/economy/story/bengalurus-economy-suffering-huge-loss-of-rs-20000-crore-anually-due-to-traffic-congestion-reveals-study-393138-2023-08-07.

person stays longer in office, they must be working harder. Long work hours are equated with sincerity, ownership and drive. They are celebrated, rewarded and expected. We love to use sarcasm, and I believe every single one of us, at some time or the other in our careers, would have heard a colleague or manager shout, 'Half-day today!' when attempting to leave the office at 6 in the evening. These cultural norms force people to sit longer and longer hours in the office, not necessarily being productive.

Another typical scene at the office is people being late to the meetings. It is almost a given that any meeting, however early you plan it, will begin later than the scheduled time because someone will come late. Most of the time, people don't even apologise, as a five- to ten-minute delay is routine. We are always expected to 'adjust, please'. This 'chalta hai', casual approach towards the clock is so deeply ingrained in us that we don't even stop to think if this is disrespectful to those who come on time. Since no disrespect is perceived, no apology is sought, and there are no negative consequences. In fact, people who arrive on time experience the punishment as they have to wait for everyone to join. This social reward of negative behaviour and punishment for positive behaviour drives a mass shift towards the former. Why should people come on time and be punished, to wait, while others join late? A better idea would be to join five minutes later. This routine is how the super-conscious clock of Indian society is ticking. Be late, because others will definitely be.

A typical day in city life starts early at 7 a.m., and if you have kids, maybe even earlier at 5.30–6 a.m., and ends by 8 or even 9 p.m. before a person gets time to retire and relax at home. Where can one find time in this personification of hustle-bustle? The commute saps energy, and long, unproductive work hours leave employees crying for the ever-elusive work–life balance. It is important to understand and reflect on these cultural expectations and harsh realities of Indian city life.

With such a cultural context, making any change to our lives and reclaiming more time for ourselves seems like a tall task. But that is where lies the opportunity. Even if we make some incremental changes in our work day, manage our habits and, more importantly, our Bright Energy, we can shine at the workplace. I won't be able to help you influence the rest of your teammates or your manager to start valuing your time, but with the experiments we will discuss ahead, you might be able to derive more out of the time you get.

Exercise: The Day Catalogue

How much influence do our community rhythms, our internal motivation and our Bright and Dark Energy batteries have on us on a typical workday? Note your activities on an average day in the table below and rate your energy levels for them in the column alongside.

Time	Activity	Activity type	Energy type	Your turn
12.00–6.30 a.m.	Sleep	Sleep	0	
6.30 a.m.	Wake up–Brush	Routine	1	
7.00 a.m.	Writing book	Passion	3	
7.30 a.m.	Writing book	Passion	4	
8.00 a.m.	Sitar practice	Passion	4	
8.30 a.m.	Coffee, chat with family	Family	4	
9.30 a.m.	Travel to office	Routine	-3	
10.00 a.m.	Travel to office	Routine	-3	
10.30 a.m.	Meeting / Work block	Work	1	
11.00 a.m.	Meeting / Work block	Work	3	
11.30 a.m.	Meeting / Work block	Work	5	
12.00 p.m.	Meeting / Work block	Work	4	
12.30 p.m.	Lunch	Routine	4	

Time	Activity	Activity type	Energy type	Your turn
1.00 p.m.	Lunch	Routine	4	
1.30 p.m.	Meeting / Work block	Work	-2	
2.00 p.m.	Meeting / Work block	Work	1	
2.30 p.m.	Meeting / Work block	Work	3	
3.00 p.m.	Meeting / Work block	Work	3	
3.30 p.m.	Meeting / Work block	Work	2	
4.00 p.m.	Meeting / Work block	Work	3	
4.30 p.m.	Meeting / Work block	Work	3	
5.00 p.m.	Evening snacks and chit-chat	Routine	4	
5.30 p.m.	Meeting / Work block	Work	3	
6.00 p.m.	Meeting / Work block	Work	2	
6.30 p.m.	Meeting / Work block	Work	2	
7.00 p.m.	Travel to home	Routine	-3	
7.30 p.m.	Travel to home	Routine	-3	

Time	Activity	Activity type	Energy type	Your turn
8.00 p.m.	Chill, Netflix	Relaxation	0	
8.30 p.m.	Chill, Netflix	Relaxation	2	
9.00 p.m.	Dinner	Relaxation	4	
9.30–11 p.m.	Chill, Netflix	Relaxation	3	

Fill in this table honestly and begin on this journey by decoding your average day. Once your chart is ready, let's proceed to the next part of the journey. We will keep referring to this chart of our day and make adjustments to it as we unravel more techniques and concepts.

Our journey began with an exploration of finding our purpose. We deep-dived into reflecting and trying to understand who we are at our core and our drivers. We then explored the inner workings of the human energy system and understood the Bright and Dark Energies at play. We reflected upon the complex relationship of Indians with time and, in that context, catalogued our day with Bright and Dark Energy intensities. On the journey of self-discovery and betterment, now would be a good time to start a deep dive into some of the biggest hurdles to being the best versions of ourselves.

- Indians have a complicated relationship with time.
- Our collectivist culture allows for a lot of laxity and ambiguity. Punctuality is not in our veins.
- Problems in cities are exacerbated by the traffic situation.
- The lax attitude towards time bleeds into the workplace, and people are often late to meetings with no remorse.
- The hierarchical structure of the Indian workplace creates issues in leaving office at will and maintaining work–life balance.
- Fill in the Day Catalogue format to plot what your typical day looks like. In the upcoming chapters we will use this information to bring changes.

CHAPTER 6

Overcoming Procrastination: The Why and How

WE HAVE ALL HEARD OF THE FAMOUS RABBIT AND tortoise parable. The confident rabbit goes to sleep, losing the race to the slow and steady tortoise. We are also familiar with the story of the ant and the grasshopper. During the summer, the ant works diligently to gather food and supplies for a harsh winter. On the other hand, the grasshopper spends his time dancing and singing, and puts off any preparation for the future. When winter arrives, the ant has enough food to survive, while the grasshopper goes hungry, freezes and has to beg the ant for help.

Both stories from Aesop's fables, the classic children's storybook, convey a powerful message to shape young kids' minds: procrastination hurts. Not doing the right activity at the right time causes harm, even death. The truth in the message of these ancient stories cannot be more evident in modern corporate life. All of us are forever found complaining about the availability of time, and in the same breath we comfortably procrastinate over all activities that we can defer.

This dual behaviour is unique to us. Despite the stories, animals do not procrastinate. We won't find them stopping work to unwind or feeling stressed with all the food hunting they have to do. We want more time and don't want to act when we have it. Despite being aware of possible future negative consequences, we postpone tasks. This behaviour is shared across the demographic spectrum. We choose to be unhappy in the future by choosing to be comfortable now.

Why Do Humans Procrastinate?

The answer lies in a complex melange of evolutionary influences and psychological factors. Procrastination is not just an issue with us managing our time but is a deeply rooted psychological problem. To explain this, let us revisit a well-known concept coined by Alasdair White, a business management theorist, to indicate our default state of mind—the comfort zone. A simple definition of the comfort zone goes something like this:

A comfort zone is a psychological state in which things feel familiar to a person, and they are at ease and in control of their environment, experiencing low levels of anxiety and stress. In this zone, a steady level of performance is possible.

Let us decode the keywords in this definition. The first is 'psychological state', which means it is a mental state that drives physical manifestations of our behaviours. Next comes the feeling of familiarity. The evolutionary reason for our mind seeking familiarity is the feeling of safety it provided to the cave dweller. If something is familiar or known, we feel secure, at ease, and in control. That is the default state we seek.

Next are the keywords of 'anxiety' and 'stress'. Anxiety is our body and mind's way of building up Dark Energy to drive some urgent reaction. It is our mind's way of signalling that something is not right, that we aren't feeling fully in control of our environment. We are feeling unsafe, and hence, we have to act to remove that factor that makes us feel safe. Fight or flight—either is fine, but action to remove the danger is a must. When you are in your comfort zone, you are not anxious, and your mind is free of the baggage of stress. With nothing blocking the mind's attention nor poking it to work on overdrive, we deliver a steady, default state of performance for any task.

The Impact of Evolution

Humans are wired to conserve energy so it can be used later when a possibly dangerous situation arises. The cave dweller had scarce resources and had to decide where to spend the precious energy gained from the severely limited food. Hence, our mind seeks all possible ways to default to the comfort zone where maximum energy is conserved. Procrastination is the human equivalent of the winter hibernation of bears. We are lazy, and so is the world. Why bother working when we can chill all day and conserve our energy to fight the next saber-toothed tiger on our tail?

Another critical thought that was constantly on the mind of Mr Cave Dweller was where he would get his food from. While some dwellers were busy plucking berries all day, others were out hunting foxes and whatnot. All that occupied their minds was where to find food and how to fill the tummy. Until we got domesticated by agriculture, food security was non-existent. Hence, the human mind was barely trained to think beyond the present moment.

Danger from predators lurking in the shadows, ready to devour at the moment's notice, made any thinking beyond today difficult, even laughable. Why think about the long term, about a year, month or even week from now, when you don't know if you will be alive then? This deep-rooted preference still influences modern human behaviour by making us choose to address immediate concerns and problems over those that might arise in the future, to prioritise short-term energy conservation and comfort over long-term planning even though it might lead to a betterment of lifestyle later.

The Impact of our Psyche

Added to these evolutionary reasons are some psychological factors that drive us to procrastinate:

Perfectionism: Perfectionists constantly strive for flawlessness and to achieve the excessively high standards that they set for themselves. While in moderation, this trait is highly beneficial to improve the quality of our deliveries, perfectionists take this pursuit to an extreme, leading to feelings of never being good enough. Striving for perfection and the almost impossibly high standards we might set for ourselves paralyse us into inaction. Perfectionists equate their self-worth with their ability to meet their unrealistic standards and end up either not starting the work or deferring it to a different day when, hopefully, their Bright Energy will take over. Enter procrastination. 'I don't feel like painting today because my muse is not musing me enough! Why even begin to paint unless you can perspective the hell out of a scene like Leo Vinci?' Perfectionists procrastinate as they feel stressed about the quality of work for a job they haven't yet begun.

Fear of failure: Humans are conditioned by society to fear failing, as that might indicate vulnerability and reduce your social status. Being vulnerable is difficult. Interactions with people at large, right from your basic appearance to your manager critiquing your work, require courage. We need the boldness to be open to feedback, to undergo scrutiny and to accept that our work has pieces that we can improve or are just plain old dud. Bringing back the three Me's of the Seed, Wolf and Jekyll, we parade the Jekyll to the world to protect our Seed and Wolf. Not all of us have the courage to expose our inner seed. The reasons for this might be our various insecurities due to our circumstances. But if we fear failure, lack confidence in our abilities and have a fragile ego, we might not even begin the work, worrying about the ridicule and pain we might face, just in case we fail. People who fear failure procrastinate as they are afraid to be bad at a job they haven't even started.

Aversion to discipline: Another factor leading to procrastination is the oft-abused word 'discipline', or our fear of it. From childhood, we have heard this word being brandished against our comfort. Children need discipline to study in school, stand in a perfect queue, play sports, keep rooms clean and arrive at classes on time, and in general, it ends up sucking the fun out of everything good in life. We begin our formative years hating discipline. If you were anything like me, you would have hated being shocked awake to attend school on a lazy winter morning when all you wanted was to cuddle up inside the blanket.

Since we hate being disciplined as children, we don't experience the multitude of benefits it brings as adults. We like to lead our lives with some routine but would gladly snooze the alarm button all day. A natural aversion to discipline and the resulting loss of focus leads us to procrastination. A lack of discipline indicates a lack of intrinsic motivation, which leads to a lack of work being done.

Affinity to rewards: One final factor leading us to procrastinate is the nature of the activity itself and the rewards, both intrinsinc and extrinsic, it provides us. If the activity is too difficult, too boring, doesn't interest us, doesn't reward us intellectually or makes us feel flooded, our mind gets super stressed, and we tend to avoid it. An overwhelming workload, which is very common in the Indian workspace, in particular, leads us to not touch even a single task.

To unwind and destress and to escape from these negative emotions, our mind's response is to seek any distraction possible. We try to distract ourselves by indulging in non-important, not urgent, but mildly more enjoyable activities. Who hasn't spent a disproportionate amount of time on the office table tennis table trying to forget the pile of work sitting at our desk?

Exercise: Track Your Procrastination

Here's a simple table you can use to track your procrastination throughout the day. The goal is to identify patterns of when, how and why you procrastinate, so you can take steps to manage and eventually reduce it.

Time of day	Task you were supposed to do	Form of procrastination (for example, social media, chatting, web browsing)	Duration of procrastination	Emotional state (for example, stressed, bored, overwhelmed)	Reason for procrastination (for example, task aversion, lack of clarity, fatigue)
6.00 a.m.–7.00 a.m.	Go to the gym	Sleep	30 minutes	Lazy	Lack of motivation
9.00 a.m.–10.00 a.m.	Write report	Scrolling Instagram	30 minutes	Bored	The task feels too big to start
11.00 a.m.–12.00 p.m.	Prepare presentation	Watching YouTube videos	20 minutes	Tired	Lack of interest in the task
2.00 p.m.–3.00 p.m.	Respond to emails	Browsing news websites	15 minutes	Stressed	Overwhelmed by volume of emails
4.00 p.m.–5.00 p.m.	Plan next week's project	Texting friends	25 minutes	Distracted	The task seems unclear

Make this table in an Excel sheet or in your journal and fill it every day for three to four weeks. This should help you understand patterns and reasons for why you procrastinate. With this context on understanding the deep-rooted causes of procrastination, we are better suited to now look into some experiments, some explorations that might help us address the root causes, and make us procrastinate less and be our whole, more productive selves.

The Five-Second Rule

Let us paint a scene. This is a cold winter morning in any Indian town. There is mist outside, and the entire landscape is sleepy. The sun is lazy, too, with a late sunrise, and has barely started warming the earth. You are dreaming in the comfort of your bed ... and are suddenly jolted awake by your cacophonous alarm, which you set to allow you to have a peaceful morning routine before you get to work.

Now, despite all your good intentions, your mind is your biggest hurdle to immediately getting out of bed. It is wired to make you feel comfortable and keep you comfortable. It is programmed to make you choose actions that conserve your energy. The basal ganglia, where all our deep memories and habits reside, is the most primitive part of the brain and runs something that, in his cornerstone book, *The Power of Habit*, the famous author Charles Duhigg calls 'habit loops'. These are deep-seated automatic responses that have been stored in our brains right from when we were born, responses or habits that occur without us knowing or becoming conscious of them. For example, shine a bright light on your eyes, and your hand will automatically come up to shade them. You complete your morning routine in an almost blank state of mind.

A brief look at the anatomy of the brain will help us understand this better. The inner lower part of the brain, consisting of the basal ganglia and amygdala, is the most primitive, ancient part where we store our habits and deep-rooted memories. It is a gift that we carry from our ancestors, and it stores within it all the learnings and reflexes that helped the cave dweller survive in harsh and dangerous conditions. Let us call it the old brain. The pre-frontal cortex, on the other hand, is a relatively newer, more evolved part of the brain that drives higher cognitive abilities like decision-making, focus, insight, judgement and memory retrieval. Let us call this the new brain.

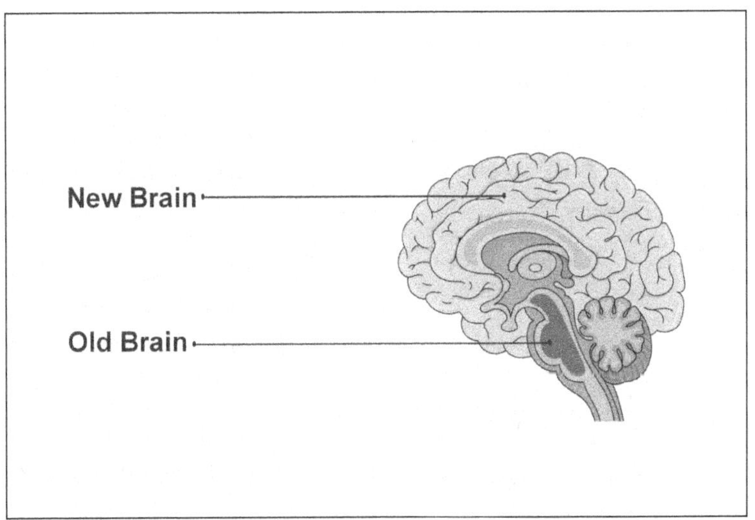

Now, when things are normal, the new brain has control, and it keeps the more basic emotions in check. Bringing back the three Me's, the new brain and Jekyll are friends. The new brain powers the Jekyll mode, and it drives our human system when things are at a default stage when in public. The new brain stores our RAM, our temporary short-term memory, to drive key actions, and keeps informing the old brain that we are safe and that the dog passing by us is friendly. Enter the stage of decision-making where we have to change from the default stage of comfort and safety to a stage of discomfort and possible risk. Now, there is a good tussle between the old and the new brain to take control and drive their respective agendas. The new brain has the idea and wants to translate that into action, while the old brain wants you to go back to the default stage of comfort, where it can keep purring like a contented cat.

Habit loops are a result of the old brain. They are very helpful for survival actions and, if harnessed correctly, can be used to create very strong, deep-rooted good habits. However, the same habit loops, when created in the mind for bad habits, create an insurmountable wall. We get literally trapped in our own brains. We know that the alarm we have set is for our own benefit; we want to get up and go to the gym or finish some chores. But the primitive brain overrides this; it inserts doubt and questions your decision. 'Why get up? It is so cozy and comfortable. Why should I need to do all the work? Today, I will relax.' We all know what we should be doing, but with all this strong talk in the mind guiding you towards comfort, it becomes very difficult to find the willpower to break the habit loop. Enter the five-second rule.

Popularised by the motivational speaker Mel Robbins, the five-second rule is a very basic yet effective activity to break habit loops. Throughout the day, we make micro-decisions. When to get up, whether to eat that ice cream or not, what to eat, whether to have that third drink, whether to yell at the kids or calmly guide them, and so on. The five-second rule is a tool that makes you act before your comfort or ease-loving brain starts to kick in and take control. It furthers us from the knowledge of whether we should or should not be doing this activity to the action of doing or avoiding it before the habit loop of procrastination, of comfort-seeking, kicks in. Before we look at the rule in action, let us briefly understand what goes on in our brain.

So when you are shocked awake by your alarm, you are facing a decision of whether to hit the snooze button or get up. The new brain has some ideas, some short-term memory stored that you had to go to the gym or get the kids ready for school and hence you need to get up. The old brain doesn't know or care about these things. That guy is more interested in humming the slow tunes and purring and wants you to take a chill pill. Voila, there is the snooze button. Zzzzz.

This might be a daily occurrence for all of us. Let's take another example of starting work on a project. Now, your new brain has short-term memory that reminds you to start the project if you have to finish it by tomorrow's deadline. The old brain suggests you wait; why spend the energy? (Even when resting, the brain uses the most energy compared to any other organ in the human body, which is about 20 per cent of our reserves; hence, conserving energy is a default). The old brain says, we have time; let's relax and do something we like instead. Let's spend our time gossiping about our colleagues and get a healthy dose of dopamine (the happiness hormone) instead. The new brain cares about the deadline, while the old brain thinks about comfort.

Research says that between the conception of an idea in the new brain and the start of the tussle with the old brain and its tricks, there is about a three- to five-second window. In this, we can break the habit loop of pressing the snooze button. This is where the five-count rule or the five-second rule comes in handy. The job is simple. As soon as you hear the alarm, you imagine a countdown from 5 to 1 and then take the action required (getting up from the bed, in this case).

A number of things happen when we count down. First, we access our short-term memory, where the numbers are stored, and this immediately awakens our new brain, the pre-frontal cortex, to take control. 5-4-3-2-1. At 1, we get a boost from a lot of conditioning: we have been hardwired to consider '1' as a prompt to act. For example, when running a race as a child, the trigger was '3-2-1 go'! It's almost as if our mind and body spring into action whenever we hear the countdown stopping at 1. This carries over to everything; a different habit loop kicks in at 1, and we spring to action and jump out of bed. The decision gets taken without active, conscious thought. You break the stay-comfortable habit loop of the old brain with a spring-into-action habit loop.

The same five-second rule can be used for all the decisions we make every day. This is a skill that can be learnt, practised and honed. Whenever you face a decision that makes you even mildly uncomfortable and your old brain starts to move you towards procrastination, recognise the pattern and, with awareness, start kicking in the five-second habit breaker. If you feel doubtful about going to the gym, start the countdown to 1; if you are feeling lazy about starting that assignment, start the countdown to 1. Simple but immensely impactful.

Eating Your Frog

Famous author Mark Twain once joked, 'If it's your job to eat a frog, it's best to do it first thing in the morning. And if it's your job to eat two frogs, it's best to eat the biggest one first.'

How often do we find ourselves deferring a critical phone call or delaying working on a crucial submission? We absorb ourselves in handling all sorts of Dark Matter. We engage in pointless chatter, kill some time on Reels, send useless emails and even start cleaning or decluttering our desks to keep our minds busy and avoid starting the most crucial task that might be either too important to fail or that takes us beyond our comfort zone.

The following experiment on overcoming procrastination is precisely what Mark Twain suggested—eating your frog! Author Brian Tracey has written a fantastic book on the concept. A simplified version is to think of your primary task of the day and do it first thing in the day. One reason to recommend doing that first thing is because our Bright Energy is the highest when our mind is well rested. We can focus better and be more creative in delivering the task when we attempt it right upon waking up.

So the next time your mind says, 'Let everyone in the office leave, and I will then sit with focus and finish this job,' don't get fooled. You might never get to it and will be so tired with the rest of the Dark Matter work during the day that you will have no Bright Energy left for this task. Don't wait for evening snacks or dinner; eat your frog during breakfast itself.

How to plan our day following this strategy? For this big one, we will bring back all our previous experiments and concepts explored!

CHAPTER 7

Planning around Purpose

IN OUR SEARCH FOR OUR PURPOSE, WE EXPLORED THE limits of our imagination across our lifetime. The eulogy helped us sharply identify the things that matter to us. We then brought the timeline closer to three years in the Odyssey technique, one year in the Happy Birthday method, and one quarter or a month in the Wheel of Life experiment. We also understood the influence of Bright and Dark Energies on our time. Associating with Bright Matter increases our Bright Energy and potential for the best utilisation of time, and Dark Matter inhibits the realisation of our potential. The energy audit of our routine day helped us understand our Bright Energy rhythms throughout the day.

Keeping all these concepts in mind, we can work on a practical application of these concepts. With this, we can make our time brighter and have a more fulfilled and happy life.

The Bright Star

The first actionable step to start living a Bright Life is to break it down to the atomic level of a key task. Let us call it the Bright Star. The Bright Star for a day is the most critical activity you plan to do. It is the task where you want to focus the most of your Bright Energy.

My journey of writing this book is an example of my personal Bright Star. On the Wheel of Life and Birthday experiments, one of the short-term targets I had set for myself is to submit the manuscript of this book. This entire exercise of researching, writing, seeking feedback, redrafting, editing, etc., needed to be done while performing well at my day job. I have to continue learning the sitar and classical music, or else I will lose my anchor. Add to this the time commitments to my family, my partner and my professional learning for career growth. I also publish weekly articles for The Foundation Project on LinkedIn, which requires its own research and writing time. There are so many balls to juggle in so little time. If we think about the demands on our time, twenty-four hours just don't seem enough.

The first step to gaining control in your life is deciding what you want control over. You have to make a choice. Not making that choice and going the way life takes you is the primary source of anxiety. Let me divide these demands on my time into some broad categories.

1. Love
2. Family
3. Work
4. Passion
5. Learning
6. Health

You may add more categories, but these six summarise the many demands on my time. Not all days will be similar; given the circumstances, my daily priorities might change. How do I then set the priorities?

Let's go deep inward. My North Star is to add brightness to people's lives and help them live the Bright Life. I want to be a People Transformation Catalyst, someone who has helped people be the best version of themselves and given a voice to those who needed it, someone who has helped people realise their full potential. To do that, I must focus on learning my HR function deeply; I must learn psychology and what drives people's behaviour. I can help people only if I can understand them. Another way to help them will be to finish this book and pass on some of what I have researched and experimented with over the past few years. If this book receives good reviews, it will be a positive reinforcement for me to build a life around my purpose.

With this clarity in mind, I am equipped to make decisions. Work is obviously essential and not a block where I want to change much. Late evening family time, dinner time and spending time with my partner are vital rituals for me to unwind and relax. These blocks freeze almost three-fourths of my waking day. Now, I have always been a morning person. Since childhood, I have gotten up early and studied for my exams. Without needing coffee or tea, my energy in the morning is decent, and I feel fresh, excited and happy.

With this context, I decided to get up a little early. Writing this book is the most important task I choose to do in a day, on my personal front; hence, it is my Bright

Star. This prioritisation has to continue till I finish the first draft. After that, I can prioritise another category, and so on. For the next few months, while daily tussles like work urgencies, health or any other urgent priority might make me decide to change the Bright Star for one day, any day, but broadly I have fixed my personal Bright Star as writing this book.

To ensure my Bright Star gets the proper focus and time, I need to reschedule my average day from the older version as seen in the table below.

Time	Old Schedule	New Schedule
6.00 a.m.	Sleep	Sleep
6.30 a.m.		Routine
7.00 a.m.	Routine	Write
7.30 a.m.	Sitar	
8.00 a.m.	Family	Sitar
8.30 a.m.		Family
9.00 a.m.	Routine	Routine
9.30 a.m.	Travel	Travel

Time	Old Schedule	New Schedule
10.00 a.m.		
10.30 a.m.		
11.00 a.m.		
11.30 a.m.		
12.00 p.m.		
12.30 p.m.		
1.00 p.m.		
1.30 p.m.		
2.00 p.m.		
2.30 p.m.	Work	Work
3.00 p.m.		
3.30 p.m.		
4.00 p.m.		
4.30 p.m.		
5.00 p.m.		
5.30 p.m.		
6.00 p.m.		
6.30 p.m.		
7.00 p.m.		
7.30 p.m.	Travel	Travel
8.00 p.m.		
8.30 p.m.		
9.00 p.m.	Family	Family
9.30 p.m.		
10.00 p.m.		
10.30 p.m.		
11.00 p.m.	Sleep	Sleep

Note that I haven't made radical changes to my routine. In my experience, radical changes, like crash diets, are not sustainable and end up backfiring instead. I have made a choice to put some family time and some sitar time on the back burner and prioritise a writing block first thing in the morning.

Now, before you judge me for sacrificing family time, I want to reiterate that generally, your family is usually the most understanding of the many demands on your time. They will gladly let you prioritise things that are important to you. Explain the project to them such that they understand what it means to you, and make an informed change in your schedule. For a few months, my family should be able to accommodate a bit less of me in the morning, especially since I have continued my dedicated, undistracted time with them in the evening.

I also had to choose between my two passions. If I reduce my sitar practice time this year, maybe I will make less progress on the different ragas I was planning to learn, but that is a decision I am making to help my chosen Bright Star. Once the manuscript is done, I have complete freedom to reinvigorate my sitar learning.

I also made just a tiny adjustment to my sleep. I advanced my wake-up time from 7 a.m. to 6.30 a.m. This minor change gave me an extra half hour in the morning, and hence, I was able to carve out a good one-hour writing block. Had I suddenly started waking up at 4 a.m. in my greed to cram more writing time, the move would have been tricky and untenable. I would have become frustrated at being unable to sustain myself and might have ended up stopping the activity entirely. Hence, remember to make only tiny adjustments to your schedule at a time.

With this focused time block, I am now able to write consistently, with sharp focus and a clear direction. When I am writing first thing in the morning, I am not thinking about the Dark Matter of emails, what awaits me at work, the day's deliveries, etc. I have not even opened my office laptop. It is a fresh start to the day, a fresh blank slate every day for me to do my deep, creative work.

Exercise: Find Your Bright Star

Answer the following three questions first thing in the morning, or the night before, and choose your Bright Star every day:

1. Want: What do I want the most important task of my upcoming day to be, which will cause a huge surge in my Bright Energy?
2. Need: What do I need to dedicate my time to in the upcoming day, failing which there will be a huge surge in my Dark Energy?
3. Value: What will add the most value in me as a person, of all the tasks in the upcoming day?

Choose your Bright Star depending on the gravity of the situation and your gut-feel assessment. The more you work to address wants and value, the better your quality of life will be.

Bright Star at Work

For the previous example, I made a personal activity the day's highlight. How would matters change if we choose a work activity as the Bright Star for the day?

For example, let's say we have a business-critical product launch in three months. If that is an important part of my goals for the year and my organisation's success depends on this product, planning for the launch will, without a doubt, be my Bright Star activity at the workplace for the next three months.

From my day catalogue done earlier, I understand that I operate with high energy and focus in three broad time blocks: early in the morning, 7–8.30 a.m., then late morning after reaching the office, 11 a.m.–12.30 p.m., and then one small spike in the evening around 4–5.30 p.m. These are the times when my focus and Bright Energy are the highest. In his pathbreaking book *Deep Work*, Cal Newport has given an excellent formula for productivity.

Productivity = Time spent x Focus

This means that if we increase our output and productivity, not just by increasing the time we spend on an activity but by how focused we are during that time, productivity will increase as well. Focus is the multiplier.

I suggest modifying the formula to bring the concept of Bright Energy into the picture because that is just important and drives your focus levels.

Productivity = Time spent x Focus x Bright Energy

= Bright Work

I feel I am the most productive when I work on my Bright Star during the blocks when my Bright Energy is the highest. This allows me to work on it with intense focus. The more the Bright Energy, the better the focus and the better the output. I like to call this Bright Work. I work best when I do Bright Work.

Keeping this formula and my Bright Energy zones during the day in mind, I want to put a time block around 11 a.m.–12.30 p.m. for my Bright Star at work. I can plan this time to be my ideation block, where I will think about ways to ensure this product launch from the example above is a success, research the competition and go through inputs to form some hypotheses of what customers want and what might work. One key aspect during this block should be action.

Now, a Bright Star work block doesn't necessarily mean that I have to work alone. I can use it for brainstorming sessions with key stakeholders and lead those meetings to generate more ideas and finalise execution plans.

An important point to note during this time block should be the lack of distractions. You must keep all the Dark Matter temptations and attractions away from you. Your focus can be sharp only if you aren't distracted by the constant calls, emails and random people knocking on your door. During brainstorming sessions, I like to get the participants' phones out to a Dark Matter sinkhole (a table with all phones deposited, on silent mode). When I am working alone, I like to put my phone in airplane mode, shut down MS Outlook for the time block to stop emails from dragging my attention away and, whenever possible, put a 'Do Not Disturb' sign on my desk and wear headphones (it doesn't play any songs, just the drone of a tanpura, but serves as a visual signal for people).

I guard this Bright Star block with my life. I block time for it in my calendar perpetually. My team members have learnt to understand and honour it, and have actually started using that block to create deep work time blocks of their own. With this block, I can be intentional 80 per cent of the time and work on my Bright Star for the day, with focus, during this ninety-minute period.

One caveat for this plan is to avoid falling into pieces when we are unable to guard the block. On the 20 per cent of days when my managers or other key stakeholders keep another meeting or discussion during this time block, I might have to let go of the Bright Star block. But all is not lost. Suppose I receive the invite for the meeting in advance. In that case, I can always move the block to the next time slot where I feel I work best, which is around 4–5.30 in the afternoon, or advance it to the start of the day at 7–8.30 a.m.

For this style of time blocking, the operative word is 'intentional'. It is far more critical that we be intentional with our time rather than sticking to a particular time block. We have to plan what we intend to do, and do it. If we cannot do that for external or internal reasons, adjusting the time of day ahead is essential to fulfill that intention. However, the best part of this system lies in its forgiving nature. Suppose you planned for a big presentation to be completed in your Bright Star block today. But your boss called for an unplanned meeting about some fires he wanted to douse. The second half of your day is also entirely blocked with non-shiftable meetings with external vendors. It is natural to get frustrated at not being able to finish your Bright Star work.

But here comes the happy twist. You can change your Bright Star. Like in the example above, there will be days when life gets in the way, and all your plans might go haywire. You still get a chance to make something else, something more within your control, the Bright Star of your day. When you return home, you can plan a good dinner with your family, or if you live alone you can prepare an elaborate dinner for yourself. You can train your mind to crave an exciting game on your PS4 once you reach home or decide that you will take your partner out for a quick night out. It can even be just watching a rerun of your favourite episodes from *Friends* with a tub of ice cream. You can shift your Bright Star to something more in your control towards the latter part of the day and feel a surge of Bright Energy during that hour. When life gives you lemons, use them with salt and tequila!

Bright Exercise: The Weekly *Bright Star at Work* Marathon

When working on an important work project, you can write the Bright Star activities for the whole week, that you intend to do on five Post-It notes and paste them on your desk.

As you keep finishing them, put a bold tickmark on the same.

It will give you immense satisfaction and an increase in Bright Energy to have a visual representation of the progress you are making on your Bright Star at work.

Day 1 Research competition.	Day 2 Submit benchmarking report.	Day 3 Research counter-measure options.	Day 4 Prepare cost comparisions of options.	Day 5 Submit final recommendations to manager.

Bright Rituals

We have discussed Bright Stars, the key highlights of our day, where Bright Energy, focus and intentional time blocks come together. But just fixing the time block on a calendar won't help sustain this habit. Habits need cues to kick them in. They need a trigger to get into action. Enter rituals.

From childhood, we have been told that cleanliness is next to godliness. Research done by Wageningen University in the Netherlands on the impact of cleanliness on employees' productivity suggests a strong correlation between the cleanliness of the work environment and the employees' perceived productivity and work satisfaction.[3] Another study suggests a strong correlation between a cluttered environment and stress. A cluttered environment is full of Dark Matter. It can never sustain Bright Energy for long.

A study by the University of Connecticut found that during periods of stress, people displayed repetitive behaviours like cleaning (remember Monica from *Friends*?)

---

3   Mirte Horrevorts, Jan Van Ophem, Paul Terpstra, 'Impact of Cleanliness on the Productivity of Employees', *Facilities* 36(2003), August 2018, https://www.researchgate.net/publication/327022122_Impact_of_cleanliness_on_the_productivity_of_employees.

because it gave them a sense of control over things.[4] Another study by Zurich University confirms the significant effect of visual clutter on visual attention, focus and performance. All this research points to the importance of a clean space in improving your focus, reducing stress and giving you a sense of control.

The first ritual that should accompany your Bright Star work is brightening up your workspace. Start with a cleaning ritual. Clear your desk of all tit-bits, rubbish and Dark Matter that should go in the bin. Keep your phones away and your pad and pen handy. If you are working on a laptop, don't have anything beside it and a pad and pen on the desk. You also need ample light. If sunlight is possible, that's best, but in its absence, ensure that the workspace is adequately lit. This routine is essential to set you into the groove to start working with focus.

The next step in setting the mood is to get some Bright Matter in. For me, a strong cup of fresh coffee or peppermint tea does the trick. The clean desk and coffee signal to my mind that it is time to sit down and start working with focus. My habit loop automatically kicks in. Voila, I am all prepped to start working on my Bright Star. This is the precise ritual that I have followed today as I wrote this paragraph and almost all of the book before this.

Sometimes, when inspiration moves me, I like adding more elements to this ritual. I love candles and flowers, and who doesn't love greenery? Especially when I am in the

---

4   Sherri Gordon, 'The Connection Between Cleanliness and Mental Health', *Verywell Mind*, 24 April 2024, https://www.verywellmind.com/how-mental-health-and-cleaning-are-connected-5097496.

mood to read a good book, I like to add some aroma in the air with some candles and move the flower vase to my study desk.

At work, this changes minutely. I do all the above, clear my desk, get coffee and put my phone away. But since that is a space with more people than my home, I also add a few more Bright Matter pieces. I put up a Do-Not-Disturb sign and put on my headphones. When all this is in place, and it takes about two minutes, my mind starts to get into the groove of doing focused work. When it comes to improving your relationship with time, mood matters.

CHAPTER 8

Motivation and Willpower

CELEBRATED PSYCHOLOGIST ROY BAUMEISTER conducted a pathbreaking experiment that is now considered as a cornerstone in furthering our understanding of human self-control.[5] The researchers asked a group of students to enter a small room individually and sit in front of a table with two bowls. One bowl had freshly baked cookies, and the other bowl had radishes. The researchers divided the students into two groups. They asked one group to eat only the freshly baked cookies without touching the radishes, and the other group had to do the opposite. While the cookie eater group had a great time, the story for the radish eaters was very different. As mentioned by some participants, they had to exert a lot of willpower to keep from picking up the delicious cookie and eat a bitter radish instead.

After the eating part of the experiment, they were each given an immensely complex, seemingly impossible puzzle to solve. The cookie-eater group approached the

---

5   Roy E Baumeister, Ellen Bratslavsky, Mark Muraven, and Dianne M. Tice, 'Ego Depletion: Is the Active Self a Limited Resource?', Case Western Reserve University, 1998, https://faculty. washington.edu/jdb/345/345%20Articles/Baumeister%20et%20 al.%20%281998%29.pdf.

puzzle with positivity. They tried the puzzle multiple times without getting frustrated and eventually gave up without being disgruntled. The cookie group tried the puzzle for an average of nineteen minutes before giving up.

The story for the radish group was completely different. From the onset, this group appeared frustrated and restless. Some muttered at the exercise's uselessness, while others just gave up and napped at the table. One person lost all his cool and started yelling at the moderator. On average, the radish group gave up in just eight minutes, a 60 per cent reduction in performance compared to the cookie group.

This experiment gives a profound insight: willpower is a finite resource. The radish group was so exhausted from exerting their willpower to stop themselves from eating cookies that they entered the puzzle part of the experiment already depleted. Conversely, those who ate cookies had their willpower intact, which allowed them to approach the puzzle in a positive and fresh frame of mind, and hence, they could use the willpower reserves to persevere longer.

This insight holds true in our daily lives, too. Difficult decisions, abstaining from sweets for a diet, navigating office politics and routine, tedious tasks like claiming reimbursements, and managing difficult conversations that demand self-discipline and control deplete the finite reserves of our willpower. Just as we feel exhausted after a strenuous workout, our willpower can get drained too.

But there is good news. Just like muscles can be trained and built, so can willpower. It is a skill that can be learnt and honed. It is a muscle that we can train and develop to handle increasingly demanding situations, and can thus be strengthened over time.

Motivation, on the other hand, is a different story. It is one of the most misused terms in the corporate world. It is a mystery; we are all trying to find the key to it. What keeps employees motivated? What will keep them running the race? What causes a shift in motivation? Why, on some days, do we feel we can win the world, while on others we can't even hold a pen? Like Bright and Dark Energies, this yo-yo of motivation happens even at different times of the day.

Now, if the motivation curve swings and is unpredictable and if willpower is a finite resource, how do we get anything done if they are the only fuel that power performance? The only correct answer is not to rely on either. To drive self-growth and bring about any positive, lasting, sustained change, a good strategy will be to move away from motivation and willpower and towards discipline and systems instead.

The Habit Builder System

To develop a system to maintain our drive to deliver, we'll need some strategies. The first step is to make the activity for which we want to build discipline enjoyable. We don't need to be disciplined to watch Netflix or eat junk food because these are inherently enjoyable tasks. We have to make some effort to make tedious, uncomfortable tasks enjoyable. How do we make efforts to be healthy fun? You can do that by adding variety. We constantly crave new stimuli as it increases our Bright Energy. Go to the gym for a few days, but pepper it up with some runs through the park and evening walks. Change the scenery every so often. A new adventure every day, and you'll keep on showing up. *Step 1, introduce variety.*

Another way to make tasks enjoyable is by doing them with a group of people who can motivate, compete, cajole and coerce each other to keep showing up. If you have a challenging exam to prepare for, get a study partner. If you want to learn a new language, find someone you can practise with. Doing things together will increase your Bright Energy and keep you going. *Step 2, find company.*

After making things fun, a good way to form discipline is to make them easy. We are such lazy beings; sometimes, even a simple task of walking for two steps to pick up the book we are supposed to be studying creates friction. We must start influencing and changing our environment to make the activity easy. If you have to go to the gym in the morning, take out your gym clothes the night before and lay them prominently in sight. To start studying first thing in the morning, keep the desk clean and prop the books and notebooks you need neatly. Reduce the friction as much as possible. To quote the great SRK in *Om Shanti Om*, make the entire world scheme to make you meet your activity goals (don't just depend on wishing for it). *Step 3, make it easy to begin.*

Now that we have made things fun and easy, it's essential to track them. We love to see progress, especially if it's visual. There are many ways to track your progress. You can use one of the many available apps to track your habits. Or you can simply cross out the days on a whiteboard. Keep the tracker visible on your desk, and refer to it daily. The visual of you showing up and doing the activity every day will motivate you intrinsically and create a virtuous cycle of you continuing to show up. *Step 4, track.*

The best way to maintain discipline is to keep challenging yourself. Nothing motivates us more than seeing ourselves grow. A marginal but significant increase or improvement after a set period will give us the satisfaction of moving forward and help start a positive feedback loop that will make our minds crave the reward. If you are trying to reduce weight by working out at a gym, every time you see the needle go down, you will get a short release of dopamine that will make you work out again and again. *Step 5, set achievable yet challenging goals.*

The Five-Step Habit Builder

I have explained the Five-Step Habit Building Exercise in the example below. Pick up one habit of your choice and fill in the table.

	Steps	Habit I want to build—Learning the sitar	Your turn
1	Introduce variety	Learn three different ragas at one time to ensure no boredom.	
2	Find company	Make friends with fellow students and practise together.	
3	Make it easy	Keep the sitar out in the living room every day as a visual reminder.	

	Steps	Habit I want to build—Learning the sitar	Your turn
4	Track progress	Make a star chart and give myself a star for every day I achieve my daily goal.	
5	Set achievable goals	Practise the sitar for a minimum of thirty minutes every day.	

Another good strategy that has worked wonders for me is putting things on my calendar. For today's knowledge workers, where our calendars run most of our lives, this is a good use of that system. What better way to induce discipline than putting the activity on the calendar and doing it during the time blocked?

In his seminal book *Atomic Habits*, James Clear describes a fantastic discipline-building technique. He says it is easiest to build habits and thence discipline for those habits by linking them with our existing habits. We all have some routines that we have followed since childhood. We all have a morning routine that helps us wake up, one that helps us start work and a night routine that helps us sleep. We have developed these routines over many years by repeating the same activity multiple times and forming strong neural connections in the brain that fire automatically, guiding you to do that activity without conscious thought.

Similarly, a good idea to introduce discipline for a new activity is to link the new habit you want to form with an existing one. Let me explain how I could develop the habit of practising the sitar daily. Taking a leaf out of our earlier examples, I formed a group with fellow learners who I can partner with. They help create a music learning mindset, we discuss Indian classical music, the nuances of various ragas, often practise together and perform monthly at a baithak, a homely concert. This group has made the sitar learning experience for me quite enjoyable.

To reduce the friction and make practising the sitar early in the morning easy, I follow a few steps, like keeping the sitar out at my designated place of practice the previous night itself. A monthly calendar that tracks how many such morning sessions I have completed, with prominent crosses marked, is visible on my desk. I get immense satisfaction looking at the many crossed-out days, proving that I have continued with the discipline for some days. Now how did I introduce the habit of practising the sitar every morning into my routine?

I have the habit of drinking a nice cup of masala tea as soon as I wake up and finish my morning brush routine. This is a routine I have been following for ages.

1.   I brush my teeth as soon as I get up at 7 a.m.
2.   I put my tea to boil.
3.   I go to the door and pick up the newspaper.
4.   I pour the tea into the cup.
5.   I take my tea to the balcony.
6.   I sip my tea as I read the news for fifteen minutes.

The best chance of building the discipline to practise daily is to introduce this habit within this deeply ingrained routine. A good strategy can be to introduce a habit stack as follows:

1.   I brush my teeth as soon as I get up at 6.45 a.m.
2.   I put my tea to boil.
3.   *I tune my sitar for two minutes.*
4.   I go to the door and pick up the newspaper.
5.   I pour my tea into the cup.
6.   I take the tea to the balcony.
7.   I sip my tea as I read the news for fifteen minutes.
8.   *I sit down in the living room and start the sitar practice.*

Just by inserting one habit of tuning the sitar for two minutes, as the instrument was prominently visible to me as I had already laid it out last night, I am now able to practise while following my deep-rooted morning routine. I have not made many changes to it, except to shift the time I wake up by fifteen minutes to get some practice time factored in. I am following the same routine that I have since a long time, but now, since I have a tuned sitar ready and learning buddies who are eagerly waiting to listen to a new piece I have tried on the raga I am learning, I find a new habit being developed. Introducing one tiny step in your deep-rooted habit loop can bring into your life discipline for a completely new habit.

This technique of habit stacking can also be used very effectively to maintain and drive up your Bright Energy during the workday. As seen in my Energy audit, my Bright Energy takes a massive dip, and my Dark Energy resurges, after the lunch hour. We all experience this. We feel drowsy after a hearty Indian meal and mostly spend the next hour or two in a dull stupor. We all have some lunch routines that we have been following.

1. I finish my meeting at 1 p.m.
2. I call my colleagues to join me for lunch.
3. I shut my laptop.
4. I pick my lunchbox.
5. I go to the place where we have lunch.
6. I chat with my colleagues.
7. I go for a short stroll/smoke break if time permits.
8. I come back and start my laptop.
9. I start my next meeting or start working on my next task at 2 p.m.

This routine is a common workplace habit that most people in India follow. After lunch, we all dread the task facing us and will gladly trade the office desk for a bed. When your body demands so much comfort, it is a significant drain on your willpower to continue working, causing low productivity during the post-lunch hours. How do we use habit stacking to take us out of this slump? By making some minor changes to the schedule above.

1. I finish my meeting at 1 p.m.
2. *I spend five minutes reviewing my day till now and note it down.*
3. *I spend five minutes reviewing the plan for the rest of the day and make changes and notes.*

4. I call my colleague to join us for lunch.
5. I shut my laptop.
6. I pick my lunchbox.
7. I go to the place where we have lunch.
8. I chat with my colleagues.
9. I go for a short stroll/smoke break if time permits.
10. I come back and start my laptop.
11. *I spend five minutes reviewing the notes made in Steps 2 and 3.*
12. I start my next meeting or start working on my next task at 2.10 p.m.

We did not make a lot of changes to this lunch time routine. We added just three new steps of five minutes each. We have not reduced our lunch time or the time for a short after-lunch stroll. But these fifteen miniutes spent in reviewing the progress till the lunch hour, planning for the second half of the day, and after a hearty lunch reviewing the priorities for the day provide immense clarity to us on how our day is going and if we are on track to achieve what we set out to. Spending these ten to fifteen minutes will add immense value to the rest of the day ahead and will help you make any changes in your plans, if needed, to deliver your Bright Star. *Step 6, build a habit stack.*

To increase the probability of deep, focused work and delivery, it would also be a good idea to look at how we can manage our energies and work to the best of our potential during the work blocks. During the workday, we are often forced to sit through meetings that go on for hours and hours, but our mind gets busy with its own flights of fantasy elsewhere. Even when working on personal projects, we start feeling restless after a certain time. The technique explained ahead is an excellent method to overcome this itch of restlessness and train our mind, and use its natural rhythms to both overcome procrastination and work with focus.

The Pomodoro Technique

The Pomodoro technique has gained popularity worldwide, with many die-hard fans and communities espousing its benefits in improving focus and productivity.

The technique was developed and popularised by Francesco Cirillo in the 1980s, when he was a university student. Like all of us, he struggled to focus and study with concentration and complete tasks. Now, many of us have used our phones or watch timers while cooking or microwave timers to heat our food. Cirillo was inspired by his tomato-shaped kitchen timer. Hence pomodoro, the Italian word for 'tomato'.

Cirillo used his kitchen timer to experiment with various durations to test his focus. To begin with, he just tested working for two minutes, followed by a two-minute break. With success, he increased the time to ten minutes, and so on until one-hour blocks. After all these experiments, he found that twenty-five minutes of intense, focused work followed by five minutes of rest was ideal for him to get the best productivity. Ten-minute intervals were too short, and sixty minutes without a break was too long. From the 1980s till today, millions of users have tried this method and swear by its effectiveness.

The Pomodoro Technique

1. Select your task.
2. Set your timer to twenty-five minutes.
3. Work on the task with intense focus for twenty-five minutes.
4. Once the timer goes off, take a mandatory break from the task.
5. During the break, try to move away from the screen or the book. Take a walk, nibble on a snack, drink some water, do some quick exercise or listen to your favourite music.
6. This thirty-minute period is called one Pomodoro. After the first Pomodoro, you repeat Steps 2 to 5. After four Pomodoros (four sets of twenty-five-minute tasks and then five-minute breaks), take a more significant break of thirty minutes.

This way, you get focused work in, with blazing Bright Energy, for an almost two-hour window, and after the thirty-minute break, you can restart from Step 2, the first Pomodoro. In a day, with the finite willpower and focus that humans are blessed with, doing two sets of four Pomodoros—that is, about four hours of focused work—has been found to be the most productive and possible. Beyond that, our focus starts to diffuse, and we start feeling more stressed. But in this focused work period of eight Pomodoros, or four hours, you would have accomplished much more than unfocused and shallow work of eight to ten hours.

The beauty of this technique is its simplicity and customisability. You can do the same experiments with the duration of the focused work and the break and find your own sweet spot. You may find that the 25–5 combination doesn't work for you and might want to change it to 30–5 or 20–10. Experiment with your phone timer and find your own Pomodoro. After all, it is easier to do and commit to just twenty-five minutes of focused work rather than staring at a scary calendar block of multiple hours. Given below is the template that you can use to plan your own pomodoros.

Time Slot		Morning Focus	Afternoon Focus
Task	Duration (Minutes)	Task 1: Project Planning	Task 2: Report submission
Pomodoro 1	25	Research	Gather all data
Break	5	Stretch your arms and back, do arm circles	Listen to your favourite song
Pomodoro 2	25	Brainstorming meeting	Write first draft, share for comments
Break	5	Hydrate with water and soothing tea	Do some desk yoga, shoulder rolls
Pomodoro 3	25	Finalise details of ideas and execution	Redraft, edit basis comments received

Time Slot		Morning Focus	Afternoon Focus
Break	5	Walk around the office, chat with a colleague	Write a gratitude note on all good things that have happened today
Pomodoro 4	25	Email batch, clear emails	Email batch, clear emails
Break	15–60	Long break– Lunch, take a walk around the office, chat with friends	Long break– Take a snack break, have some watercooler chat

Now, with a deeper understanding of willpower and motivation and some experiments on overcoming procrastination under our belts, let us shift our attention to another major derailer of our time: having too much on our plate and not knowing what to finish first. In the upcoming section, we'll look at various strategies to help us prioritise tasks, conserve and manage our Bright Energy and reclaim time.

- Willpower is a powerful but finite resource.
- Just like muscles, it can be trained to increase its capacity.
- Motivation is extremely volatile and susceptible to minute fluctuations in our environment.
- The key to sustained motivation is to build reliable, Bright systems.
- The five-step programme to build a Bright system of motivation:
  1. *Introduce variety*: Counter boredom by mixing tasks.
  2. *Find company*: Doing tasks together with people and holding yourself accountable generates motivation.
  3. *Make it easy*: Reduce friction to a minimum so that starting the task is easy. Once begun, it is easier to go on. Managing to start is the key.
  4. *Track*: Seeing progress visually creates a virtuous cycle to keep going.
  5. *Set achieveable yet challenging goals*: A state of flow is achieved when we feel sufficiently challenged. A belief of eventual achievement of the goal is required to not be intimidated and procrastinate.
- Bright Habit Stacking: Insert the layer of new habits that you want to form between the steps of already formed strong habits.

- The Pomodoro Technique:
  - Complete your tasks in batches of thirty minutes, with twenty-five minutes dedicated to work and five minutes to unwinding.
  - In one batch, do four sessions of Pomodoro of thirty minutes each and then take a break of at least thirty minutes.
  - In a day, people can do at most two such batches of four Pomodoros. Beyond that, it's impossible to maintain the focus, and our Bright Energy reserves decline.

CHAPTER 9

Prioritisation with Precision

WE ALL HAVE DAYS WHEN WE STARE AT UNENDING TO-do lists, scratching our heads on what to begin with and reminiscing about long-lost days when life was easy. With the exponential growth of the Indian economy, all corporations are trying to get a share of the winnings. This translates into an ever-increasing demand on employees to be more productive, deliver more in less and improve quality while constantly reducing costs. This strain on margins also has an effect on our work lives. Most teams are understaffed, and business leaders don't add resources until the existing ones start burning out or results are threatened. This increasing demand directly correlates with the quantum of work we have. Madness everywhere!

To establish some method in this madness, understanding what matters becomes vital. Knowing priorities and being able to prioritise are essential. In this chapter, we will try some experiments on prioritising work and see what works for you. All the suggestions have their own fans, and I encourage you to try them all first before zeroing in on what works best for you.

The Money–Energy (ME) Matrix

The first prioritisation technique is a matrix that I have created to manage my priorities on any regular day, and it has helped me immensely to make better decisions.

Let us start by plotting a simple two-by-two diagram. On the X-axis, we put Bright Energy; on the Y-axis, we plot the potential monetary benefit of any activity. The resulting framework is what I like to call the Money–Energy (ME) Matrix, which showcases visually all my tasks on the scale of their Bright Energy release and the monetary impact they have on my life.

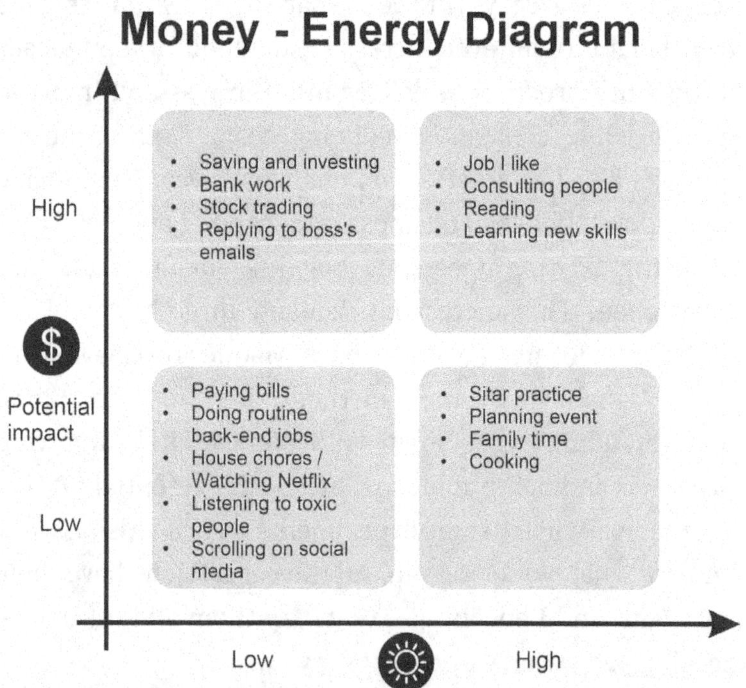

The four quadrants are as follows.

The Eagles: The high energy, high potential quadrant. This consists of activities where I feel my Bright Energy shoot up and those that significantly impact my current or future earnings. These activities create Bright Matter for me, which also translates into money. Examples of this, for me, are some parts of my role as the HR head of one of the business units of a real estate company. Do I like all parts of my job? No. But certain parts of my job, like facilitation, conducting workshops, managing rewards, talent management, consulting people, building careers, etc., make my day bright. If I perform well in these aspects, it will mean good rewards and potential monetary impact in the form of continued employment, increments and role elevation opportunities.

As humans, seeing ourselves grow is immensely satisfying; hence, we feel our Bright Energy shoot up when we invest in our personal growth. It also creates Bright Matter, which we will be able to encash at a later date, creating future monetary potential. Learning new skills like designing workshops, doing research, decoding psychology and human motivation, understanding leadership philosophies, etc., all increase my skills as an HR professional. In my opinion, the time spent learning these skills is spent well.

One of the habits I have picked up over the last few years is reading voraciously. I have read some thought-provoking and life-changing books that have helped reshape my philosophy for leading a good life, made me a better person and a better professional and positively impacted all my relationships. This has led to a virtuous circle of creating Bright Matter through reading.

Writing is a relatively newer activity that I have picked up, and I feel it crystallises the sea of ideas in my mind into a lucid narrative on paper. It is a great way to solidify learning and ideas and gain clarity of thought. It helps me express myself to the world and spread some goodness. That led to me writing this book, which turned out to be a good source of Bright Matter creation. These are a few of my Bright Matter-generating activities, and I urge you to make a grid of your own and note yours down. It is a no-brainer that we should dedicate 80 per cent of our time to these activities on a typical workday. These activities bring you happiness and money (that can't buy you happiness, but it won't hurt, will it?) Whenever you have to take a call between slotting two different activities on your calendar, always prioritise the activity that falls in this high energy/high monies quadrant.

The Puppies: Let us look at the high energy, low monetary impact quadrant. These activities generate Bright Energy sparks but do not translate into any significant financial impact. For most people, these activities involve spending time with their loved ones, practising their hobbies and generally enjoying themselves. For me, it is cooking with my partner, playing cards with my family and hosting and attending parties with friends, all activities that make me happy without causing a significant impact on my wallet, both positively and negatively. Another Bright Energy activity for me is doing my riyaaz on the sitar. It is a purely creative and therapeutic activity for me, and while I perform for friends and fellow learners, this is not an activity that will turn into some side hustle. Hence, this goes in the high Bright Energy and low monetary impact quadrant.

Now, these activities are significant. They are essential to recharge our Bright Energy batteries. They build the foundation on which we are then able to create the Bright Matter of the first quadrant activities. If we don't take enough time for these recharging activities, we won't be able to spend time fruitfully in the activities that help us earn money. I set 80 per cent of my time on weekends aside for them. During weekdays, almost 20 per cent of the time that remains after the quadrant one activities goes into these as well.

The Leeches: This quadrant comprises low Bright Energy and low monetary impact activities. These diminish our Bright Energy and bring out Dark Energy. They feel like a burden to me, and I try to avoid them as much as possible. Who likes to remember to pay electricity or gas bills, claim reimbursements on portals, file documents, do routine paperwork or household chores? We all have a substantial administrative overhead that eats up a lot of our time.

I agree with the author Cal Newport that if you can afford it, pay someone else to do these jobs, so that you can spend that time doing something you love. Automate your bill payments. Delegate the routine back-end jobs to an operations team. For house chores, get help. Newport suggests setting up an hourly rate for yourself, depending on your earnings. Let's say it's ₹1,000/hour. This is the value of your time. Now, for any activity that you can pay someone else to do at a cheaper rate, say ₹100/hour, it makes sense to free up that time and invest it in doing something from quadrant one or two.

In this quadrant, I also placed activities that create Dark Matter—useless, aimless pursuits that drain our time. Doom-scrolling on social media, binge-watching Netflix and TV, constant chatting on WhatsApp or excessive and obsessive emailing are all activities that bring out our Dark Energy. While they may not have a significant and immediate monetary impact, they do leave us feeling guilty and unfulfilled, and make us wonder: where did the time vanish? These are activities that we should avoid altogether.

Time spent with toxic friends and relatives also goes in this quadrant. Idle gossip also lands in quadrant three. Gossip was developed as a pro-social activity to highlight the shortcomings of various members of society so that we could make intelligent, informed connections. But its true nature is inherently negative. Whoever gossiped about someone's good qualities? Hence, gossip is an activity that creates Dark Energy and is best avoided.

We must re-evaluate toxic relationships or friendships, too, even if long-lasting. These bring out a massive surge in Dark Energy and sap us of the joie de vivre. Reflect, act and reallocate the time you spend here.

The Termites: The fourth quadrant comprises activities that generate low Bright or even low Dark Energy but have a high monetary impact. These activities might sap us of our energy, but, if left uncompleted, can have significant monetary impact. I find anything related to banks and finance highly dull. It is one area where I have been unable to find any joy. Anything related to investing, trading, banking and savings is a snooze-fest. Year-end tax and returns filing is the icing on this boredom cake. But despite that, they have a significantly high monetary impact.

Hence, I have to force myself to find time to do these activities. Automating them through an investing app or your bank relationship manager is the best option. You may hire experts to invest and trade for you if you can afford it. However, the bottom line is that these are unavoidable, high monetary impact activities for which one must take time out.

Some other examples of low energy, high monetary impact activities include reviewing and documenting contracts, understanding legal risk and mitigation. But for me, one of the highest Dark Energy-creating activities is replying to emails. Emails from your superiors, your managers and leaders demanding vital information, and from your team members asking for approvals need to be answered, and, if not done correctly in time, can lead to lower job performance and, hence, a potential high monetary impact. Therefore, we must allocate some parts of the workday to this low-energy, high-impact activity block.

Now that we have understood the four quadrants of Bright Energy/Monetary Impact potential activities, we can decide how to split our time. During the work week, Monday to Friday, our ME matrix will look different than the one on weekends. I recommend having Eagles and Puppies take up the most space on the average day, followed by Termites, and the least amount given to Leeches. My ME matrix on weekdays looks like this.

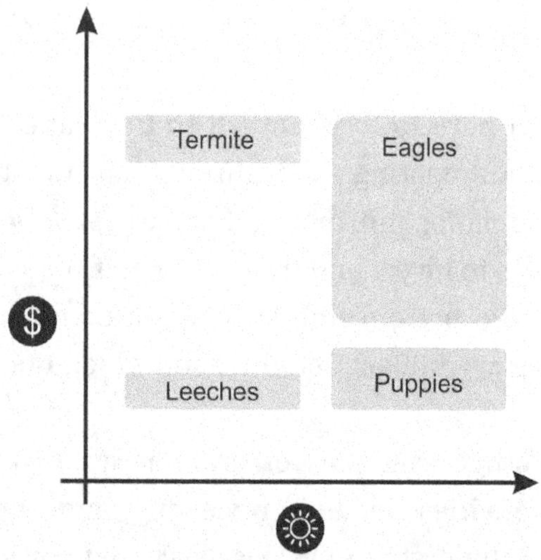

But on weekends, my ME Matrix shifts, and with far greater time being given to Puppies, it looks a bit like this:

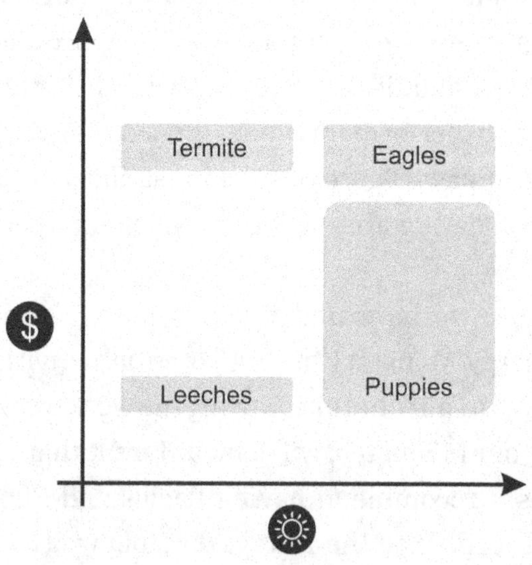

This ME matrix is a simple tool I use to plan my time blocks during the week. To understand this with another lens, let us look at a possible ME matrix for a salesperson.

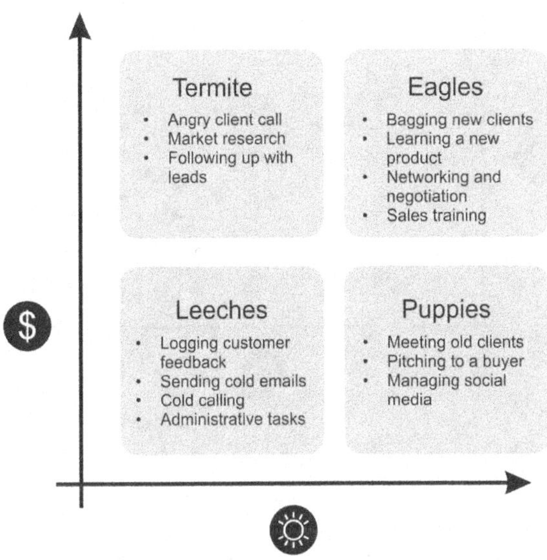

Bright Exercise: Make Your ME Matrix

In the diagram below, put down your tasks that are Eagles, Puppies, Termites and Leeches. Break the aspects of your job into associated tasks. Then, plot them on the ME matrix to understand what part of the job gives you joy and adds to your monetary potential. Maximise that portion while you try to delegate those aspects that sap your energy and deliver no or less monetary impact.

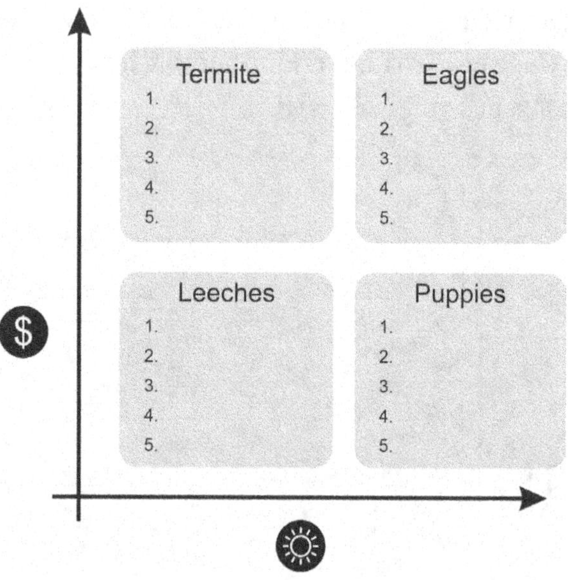

The Eisenhower Matrix

Dwight D. Eisenhower said, 'Who can define for us with accuracy the difference between the long and short term! Especially whenever our affairs seem to be in crisis, we are almost compelled to give our first attention to the urgent present rather than to the important future.'

Eisenhower was the thirty-fourth president of the US and a celebrated veteran of World War II. During his eight-year presidency, the US made many pathbreaking strides, such as the creation of NASA, the incorporation of Alaska and Hawaii into the union, the construction of the Interstate Highway, the end of the Korean War and the signing of the first draft of the Civil Rights Act. Given the number and stature of his achievements and contributions, one can deduce that he was a very productive person.

In 1954, he quoted a friend in a speech, 'I have two kinds of problems, the urgent and the important. The urgent are not important, and the important are never urgent.'

This quote formed the basis of the eponymous Eisenhower matrix, an important time management and prioritisation tool. The quote above divides any problem or activity into two axes: urgency and importance. Let us briefly decode these two words.

Time is at the forefront of an *urgent* task. It must be completed immediately, and a delay can damage the 'whole' of which this task is a part.

Impact is at the forefront of an *important* task. This task impacts your objectives and must be completed to achieve any significant progress in your objectives. Failure to do this important task will make it impossible for you to achieve your goal.

With these clear definitions, the Eisenhower matrix divides the tasks into four dimensions. The salesperson example can help us understand how the Eisenhower matrix helps make decisions.

- *The important and urgent*: Do it. These are tasks with clear, urgent deadlines and immense consequences if not finished on time. Examples include submitting a project for the client, responding to your boss's email with the required data, picking up your kid from school and visiting the dentist for a toothache. For the salesperson, activities like a closing call with a prospective client, attending to an angry client, meeting monthly sales targets and responding to high-priority leads will form the 'Do It Now' category.

- *The important but not urgent*: Schedule it. These tasks are essential for long-term success and bring you closer to your goals but don't require immediate action. We can schedule these tasks for a future time, but we should be aware that this makes procrastinating very easy. Examples include formulation of long-term strategy, brainstorming for an execution plan, networking with stakeholders, investing in self-skill development and exercising to keep healthy. For the salesperson, market research to develop competition understanding, building a strategic plan to achieve quarterly targets and attending sales training and workshops will form the 'Schedule It' category.

- *The urgent but not important*: Delegate it. These tasks must be done quickly but don't require your specific skill set. You can outsource these routine, back-end and administrative tasks. Examples include answering unnecessary phone calls, organising office events and attending family functions. For a salesperson, uploading call logs, data entry requirements, coordination of logistics for an event, replying to minor customer queries and scheduling urgent follow-up meetings would form the 'Delegate It' category.

- *The not urgent and not important*: Delete/eliminate it. These tasks provide little value and must be eliminated to free up time to do more tasks from the urgent and important category. For a salesperson, these include all those meetings that could have been emails, unnecessary calls, follow-ups from others asking for data, replying to a massive pile of emails, personal errands, browsing social media and eating junk food. All these activities and distractions during a workday should form the 'Eliminate It' category.

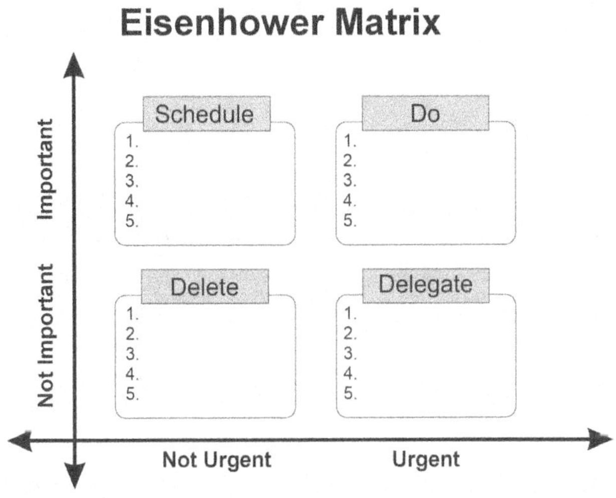

The Eisenhower matrix is a simple but effective tool for prioritising our workday. Ideally, we should spend most of our time on quadrant two, schedule activities that help us achieve our long-term goals but can be closed at our own pace. We need to give the first priority to the first quadrant, the 'do it now' category, as we will suffer if we don't meet those deadlines, but the endeavour should be to work in a manner that fewer activities reach the urgency phase. For the not important but urgent category, you should be assertive to minimise these urgent distractions and, wherever possible, delegate them. It would be best if you tried to eliminate quadrant four activities. These are distractions that lead you to feel worse later.

Bright Exercise: Fill the Eisenhower matrix for your tasks in the format below.

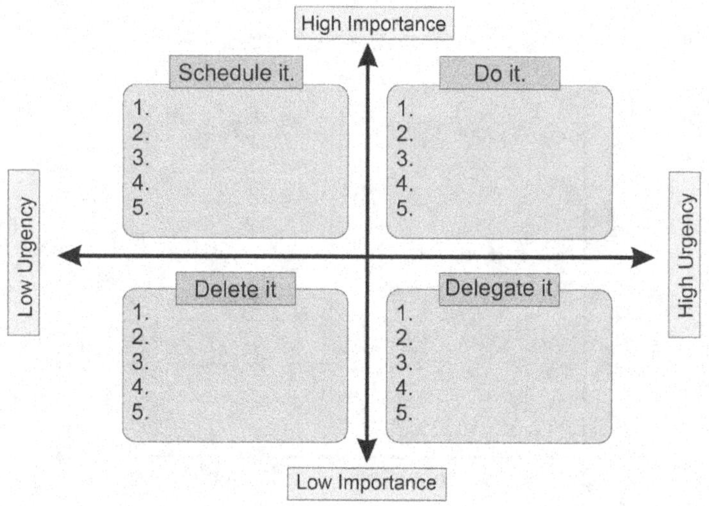

The ME matrix and the Eisenhower matrix are my primary tools for prioritising my day and week. I also use these tools to help put in order the workflow of my team so they know what urgent and important priorities we all need to focus on. Now, let us look at some more techniques that you can use to prioritise your day.

Other Prioritisation Techniques

The ABCDE Method

A straightforward yet effective method of planning and prioritising all the activities you have to deal with during a workday is to divide them into five categories: ABCDE. There are two steps in implementing this method.

Step 1: Prepare a comprehensive list: Make a list of all the tasks you want to complete in the day. Ensure the list is thorough.

Step 2: Task categorisation: Use the metrics in the guide below to assign a priority category to all these tasks, ranging from A to E, depending on their urgency and importance.

Category A: Very important/ Major consequence. These tasks are extremely urgent and important and will significantly impact your day or life if not done. They demand immediate attention. For example, getting back to your boss with a report for her upcoming presentation today. These are your frogs and must be eaten first thing in the day, with utmost focus.

Category B: Important/minor consequence. These tasks will be of good value to you in the medium and long term and bring you closer to your goals. The urgency for these tasks is a bit lower, and you can survive even if they are not closed today. For example, planning for a critical product launch next quarter is an important task, but it doesn't have the same level of urgency.

We must only start a Category B task once all Category A ones are closed. You should not be distracted by a tadpole if you have a frog waiting for you.

Category C: *Nice to do/ no consequence.* These are tasks that are nice to do but are not pivotal to your immediate or mid-term future objectives. They will not have any consequences if they are not completed today. You do these tasks to unwind or enjoy and balance your heavy professional workload. Examples include networking, coffee with friends and colleagues, organising office potlucks, etc.

As a rule, we can only begin a Category C task once we have completed every single Category A and B task.

Category D: *Delegate.* Occasionally, we have to do some activities that are better assigned to someone else. The rule is to delegate everything we can to others to have time to do our Category A activities. Examples include driving to work, filing tax returns, submitting reimbursement claims, doing house chores and back-end administrative work. If you can afford it, delegate.

Category E: *Eliminate.* We all have tasks that add zero value to our objectives, not even administratively. It would be best to eliminate all these time-sucking, Dark Energy-creating activities that become obstacles to dedicating your time to category A/B/C activities. We must learn to say no to tasks that add zero value to our lives.

We often find ourselves busy all the time but still end the day with some hugely important tasks pending and a feeling that we haven't achieved anything. To avoid addressing the important task, we often decide to finish all the small administrative work first and make ourselves believe that we will attack the most important task later in the day, only to find that we have no motivation, interest or Bright Energy left for it. This phenomenon is called 'productive procrastination'. The ABCDE method is brilliant for avoiding it. It forces us to eat the frog first.

The 1-3-5 Method

The 1-3-5 method is a variation of the prioritisation techniques we have discussed. It recommends that after we have made a list of tasks we intend to work on for a day, we should first focus on the most challenging and most urgent one first. Only after eating the frog should we proceed to the following three tasks with medium importance. Now, we can mix the Pomodoro technique here and do the following three tasks using the Pomodoro method: three slots of 25+5 minutes each. The last part is doing five administrative tasks. We can club these tasks together at the end or pepper them intermittently along with the three medium-importance tasks.

For our salesperson example, the frog task can be giving a big presentation to a potential client. She should prioritise this during the first part of the day. Once she completes the most important presentation task, she can finish three medium tasks: analysing past purchase trends, working on the presentation due next week and calling some old clients to convert them into hot leads. The five administrative tasks like uploading call logs on the system, writing a memo about the pitch given in the morning, sending an email update to the manager, scheduling the next client's meeting on the system and calling her aunt on her birthday can all be finished in one batch together at the end of the day.

The Zeigarnik Effect

While sitting in a restaurant in Vienna, German psychologist Kurt Lewin made an interesting observation. He noticed that a server remembered the details of an unpaid order far more easily. Until the order was paid, the server would remember all the details, but once the payment was made, he would have trouble remembering its contents.

Lewin's student and Soviet psychologist Bluma Zeigarnik then designed some experiments to further deep-dive into this observation. She gave students simple puzzles, maths problems and tasks like putting beads together. Half the students were interrupted partway through the task. After waiting an hour, she asked the participants what they were working on. Interestingly, she discovered that people who were interrupted in their tasks were twice as likely to remember their task compared to those who had solved the puzzles and completed the task.

This experiment led to some very interesting postulations. Human short-term memory works very similarly to that of computers. We have limited space for information storage in our RAM (random access memory of computers). When a task is unfinished, like in the case of the server, when the order is unpaid, his livelihood depends on remembering its contents. Until the payment is made, even though the server is busy taking other orders and bringing them to the tables, he is making a conscious and sometimes unconscious effort to recall the data of the unpaid order in the short-term working memory. Once the payment is made, the effort to hold that data in short-term memory is unnecessary, as he has to replace it with data about other live orders. So he releases that data to make space for the next important item. This selective storage and bringing back of tasks to short-term memory is unique for unfinished tasks, and this phenomenon is called the Zeigarnik effect.[6]

We experience this effect more than we realise. We have all found ourselves thinking about some unresolved issue at work, some challenging problem we have been grappling with or even dreaming about some vital issue we aim to tackle. Due to the Zeigarnik effect, previously unfinished tasks will creep into your memory even when you have moved on to other tasks.

The ramifications of this effect help us arrive at *the two-minute rule*. The idea was popularised by David Ellen, who in his seminal work *Getting Things Done*, postulates that as soon as we get a task that we can finish in a two-minute window, we should do so and then move to other tasks. This is essential, because if we have already been distracted by this two-minute job, the mental tension and effort to keep our mind focused on the main task will be too much. We will constantly be thinking about this small unfinished task and be unable to focus on the main task.

---

6   Kendra Cherry, 'The Zeigarnik Effect and Memory', *Verywell Mind*, 1 January 2024, https://www.verywellmind.com/zeigarnik-effect-memory-overview-4175150.

Let us say you are preparing for an important presentation and get a call from your food delivery person. Ideally, it would be best if you had handled these notifications before sitting down for the focused work block, but now, since this call has already broken your concentration, you will need to refocus your mind on the task. You are presented with two choices. Either ignore the call and let the person deliver at the apartment's main gate and collect it later, making an effort to go to the main entrance, or answer the call, give directions and resume the work.

If you choose to not take the call, you are probably entering a lose-lose situation. The fact that the food box is now lying at the apartment's main gate and that you need to go and pick it up will now be playing at the back of your mind. Another possibility is that you might start wondering about the reason for the call itself: maybe the delivery partner called because part of my favourite order wasn't available, and he cancelled my order. If my order is cancelled, how will I eat? Let me check the app, see the order status, etc. You will notice an immediate increase in your Dark Energy because of the anxiety and indecision.

If you take the call, you understand that he has reached the foot of your building; you give him the code to come up and instruct him to leave the bag outside your door without ringing the bell. You have closed this small task within two minutes, and now, with some sense of a mental tick box congratulating you on successfully arranging your lunch, you can now focus entirely on the task at hand.

This is a small example of how the two-minute rule comes into play, but it very clearly elucidates the long-lasting negative effect it can have if not followed. Hence, if you have been distracted by becoming aware of an urgent two-minute task, it is better to finish it and only then proceed. By doing this, you will be able to save a lot of cognitive tension and loss of productivity, and save yourself from a surge of Dark Energy.

As a result of all the explorations in this chapter, we have arrived at a few ways to schedule our day. To get the best out of these arbitrary lines on a paper that we have drawn, showcasing our intended usage of time, we need to know how to focus and cancel noise, and tap into our Bright Energy battery to create Bright Matter. Only when we create Bright Matter do we use the time well. Let us look at some strategies for working with focus and brightness.

- Prioritisation is key to improving our relationship with time.
- The ME Matrix: Plot your tasks on a framework with Bright Energy on the X-axis and potential money impact on the Y-axis. This divides the tasks into four types:
  1. The Eagles: These cause an increase in our Bright Energy and have significant monetary impact. These must be our top priority on weekdays.
  2. The Puppies: These cause an increase in our Bright Energy but do not have any monetary impact. We must prioritise these on weekends and at home.
  3. The Termites: These decrease our Bright Energy but have significant monetary impact. These need to be completed after the Eagles and Puppies.
  4. The Leeches: These are huge drains on our Bright Energy and have no monetary impact; they must be removed from our list.
- The Eisenhower Matrix: Plot your tasks on a framework with their level of urgency on one axis and importance on the other. This divides the tasks into four types:
  1. Q1: High urgency and high importance—These must be prioritised above all other tasks.
  2. Q2: Low urgency but high importance—These are the solid building blocks. These must receive maximum time allocation.

3. Q3: High urgency but low importance—These tasks must be delegated to others.

4. Q4: Low urgency and low importance—These tasks must be deleted from your to-do list and avoided.

- ABCDE Method: Divide tasks into five categories. First finish category A and only then move to B and then C. D tasks should be delegated to others and E should be eliminated.
- 1-3-5 Method: Create batches of one big task, three medium tasks and five administrative tasks.
- The Zeigarnik Effect: Unfinished tasks will be stored in your working memory for the short term, even if you have moved on to other tasks.
- The Two-Minute Rule: Any task that takes just two minutes to be finished must be completed before moving on to any other task.

CHAPTER 10

Working with Focus and Brightness

WINIFRED GALLAGHER, IN HER BOOK *RAPT*, WROTE, 'Your life is a sum of what you focus on.'

We have dedicated the earlier parts of the book to finding more time at the correct time of day to do our best work and create Bright Matter. But how to make the best use of the time block we have created to ensure we have the best output possible?

To recap, the formula for productivity that we discussed in our chapter on Bright Stars is

$$\text{Productivity} = \text{Time spent} \times \text{Focus} \times \text{Bright Energy} = \text{Bright Work}$$

While we have discussed at length the importance of Bright Energy and its strong correlation with the time spent being more productive, let us now look at the other part of the equation: focus. Even if our Bright Energy is high and we spend the time allocated to a particular activity, if we don't do it with focus, our net productivity will be diminished, tending towards zero. Here are some common mistakes that reduce focus.

What Makes Us Lose Focus

We have all had days when we can't bring our minds to focus on anything. It happens not necessarily when we are stressed but also when we are too happy, excited or bored. I don't think I would be wrong to say that the default state of the human mind is to be unfocused and responsive to all stimuli. This behaviour might be rooted in our need for survival, which required cave dwellers to constantly look for danger and, hence, not spend too much time focusing on any single stimulus.

Whatever the origins, the modern knowledge worker finds it hard to maintain focus for a long time. Some of the causes are discussed below.

Twiddling Thumbs

The first reason for being unable to focus is not knowing what to focus on. We are not all efficient planners. We don't maintain effective schedules. Hence, when we have some time but no plan on how to spend it and no demand out of that period, we lose focus. The most typical manifestation of this is doom-scrolling on social media. First thing in the morning, without even being fully awake, our hands go to our phones and tap-tap-tap on Instagram, Facebook or WhatsApp. The same happens whenever we find ourselves bored through the day. We have been programmed to default to social media mode so that we don't have to face the demands of reality.

The first step to improving focus is to know and plan what we want to do with the time available. It would be helpful if we had some SMART goal—a specific, measurable, achievable, relevant and time-bound objective for that specific period of time. If you know the desired outcome from that hour, you will find it easier to focus and to keep bringing back your focus to the task at hand in case the mind wanders.

Volatile Emotions

While we are highly emotional and extremely aware creatures, we face a fundamental issue: we experience emotions and awareness predominantly in two different brain parts. Remember the diagram of the human brain from earlier? We feel emotions primarily in the limbic system, the old brain, while the new brain, the prefrontal cortex region, drives our awareness. Now, these two parts of the brain do not talk to each other a lot, which means they haven't developed powerful neural connections, and hence, while we feel an emotion, we aren't necessarily aware of the kind of emotion we are feeling.

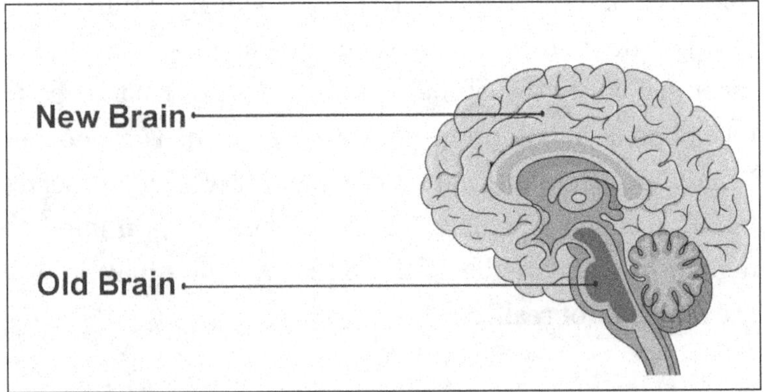

Even if we reflect and become aware of the emotion we are feeling, we don't have access to information about what causes that emotion. We have all experienced irritation and anger, but becoming aware of that feeling a bit later. The cause takes a little longer to identify.

Emotions are hard. Acknowledging and understanding them is even harder. When we are trying to focus, emotions, especially negative ones, can be a significant derailer. Assuming we have crossed the first hurdle of being intentional with our time with the methods from the previous chapters, we now have a time block earmarked for doing some serious, focused work. You have a super important presentation coming up, for which you need to prepare, but you're very anxious about it. Will you be able to focus well? I doubt it.

Not just this, let's say the work you have earmarked for this time block is particularly challenging, and you're riddled with doubt about your ability to succeed. Many times, we don't decode these feelings. We have difficulty focusing but aren't sure why. Next time that happens, try to decode the root cause of your emotional state. Is it anxiety, boredom, self-doubt or some other fear of failure that is distracting you? Once you decode the emotion, reflect and understand what might be causing it and try to deal with the cause before you attempt to restart the work.

Our mind loves to avoid working on complex tasks and escape to the distractions of Dark Matter, such as checking messages and doom-scrolling, instead of tackling the real cause of distress. Your mind will play tricks to escape the tension; it will push you to look at just one message, watch just one episode of *Friends*—anything to ignore the negative emotions and soothe your anxiety instead of resolving it. Don't give in. Decode what you are feeling and why you are feeling it, and fix the root cause.

The Attention Residue

In the previous section, we discussed the Zeigarnik effect of how our brain remembers unfinished tasks by recalling them to the pre-frontal cortex, or the aware, short-term memory to keep it fresh and accessible. But what happens to this memory when we are running from meeting to meeting on a typical workday?

Research done by Microsoft Research Lab asked some people to attend meetings wearing EEG equipment to monitor their brain activity.[7]

Each subject was asked to attend two different kinds of meeting sessions over two days. In one session, they were asked to participate in four back-to-back meetings without any break in between. In the second session, the next day, they could take a ten-minute break between each meeting. When the participants did so, they felt a low level of stress. On the other hand, when they had to attend meetings back to back, they felt a sustained build-up of stress levels with each passing meeting.

This experiment clearly shows one key aspect of our brain. As we move from one meeting to the next, from

---

7   Greg McKeown, 'To Build a Top Performing Team, Ask for 85% Effort', *Harvard Business Review*, 8 June 2023, https://hbr.org/2023/06/to-build-a-top-performing-team-ask-for-85-effort.

one task to the next, our brain doesn't immediately make the switch to the new one. While our body might be in the next meeting, working on the next task, some part of our brain continues to think about the previous one. This is the concept of *attention residue*, a term coined by celebrated psychologist Sophie Leroy in her seminal paper on the challenge of switching between tasks.[8]

Attention residue is the continuance or persistence of cognitive activity about task A even when one has moved to task B. It happens if we don't take a break between the two tasks; even if we have finished task A, our brain will continue to dwell on it while we move to task B. Attention residue is a key focus destroyer. It isn't easy to concentrate on one task if you have some other one singing carols in your mind. The more you switch tasks back to back, the more the build-up of attention residue, the greater the stress, and the less the focus. The Microsoft experiment shows that even a ten-minute break from this task switching can break this chain build-up. The Pomodoro technique applies this understanding beautifully. Do your task for twenty-five minutes, and before you begin the next, take a break for five minutes to remove the attention residue from your brain.

---

8   Sophie Leroy, 'Why Is It So Hard To Do My Work? The Challenge of Attention Residue When Switching between Work Tasks', *Organizational Behavior and Human Decision Processes*, 109(2), July 2009, https://www.sciencedirect.com/science/article/abs/pii/S0749597809000399.

Bright Experiment: The Single-tasking Day

At work, try to live two kinds of days.

Day 1: The Multitasking Day: Try to complete multitasking today. Juggle calls, type emails as you are on call, be on WhatsApp while talking to someone.

Day 2: The Single-tasking Day: Do only one task at a time today. Keep your phone out of reach for minimal distraction. Put a 'do not disturb' sign on your desk and your headphones on. Go to the next task only after you have finished your current task. Take a break in Pomodoro style.

Note down the following aspects for both days:

1. Stress levels: 1 to 5

2. How productive you felt: 1 to 5

3. Your productivity for the day (with inputs from your manager and colleagues)

4. Task completion time.

Let empirical evidence drive your decision on whether multitasking or singletasking works better for you.

Kitkat Breaks

Even though it sounds like an oxymoron, taking a break from work can do wonders to increase your focus. Breaks allow our brain to decompress, release the enormous payload it was placing on our metabolic energy and pause the neurons that were firing away in a frenzy during the focus workblock. Planning the break properly for the right duration and doing the right kind of activity is essential. If you make the break too long, you might find returning to the same rigour challenging. If you make the break too short, you won't feel refreshed, defeating the purpose. If you take breaks too frequently, you won't be able to get into the groove and deliver your best work. If you take the break after too long, you risk burnout and exhaustion. Each of us has to do some intentional experiments and find our rhythm of deep, focused work and break periods.

Another critical point to note is that during this break, we shouldn't get engrossed in our phones or other digital entertainment like social media, as that doesn't allow the brain residue to drain. The break should also mean time away from digital gadgets. Instead, we can take a brisk walk, chat with friends, meditate, do minor stretches, exercise or take a quick nap—anything that can help us reset and feel rejuvenated. With attention residue gone, we should be able to renew our focus on the task at hand.

Sleepless Bright Energy Battery

Sound sleep is essential to recharge our Bright Energy reserves. When we sleep, our entire body relaxes, our systems slow down, our body restores itself, and we build reserves of energy to utilise for the rest of the day. A minimum of six to eight hours of sleep, depending on our sleep cycles, is a must for us to maintain the necessary reserves of Bright Energy. If we don't have those reserves, we will feel exhausted, depleted and disinterested in the day's tasks. Our Dark Energy will rise, making us lose focus. We will try to escape the task and prefer to rest instead. A sound body leads to a sound mind, and you need sound sleep to achieve a sound body. The better your sleep quality, the better your focus will be the following day.

How to Improve Focus

We have all heard the famous story of the warrior Arjuna and the bird from the Mahabharata. Arjuna's guru asks the class to aim at a toy bird in a tree and asks each one of them what they see. They all describe the tree, the bird, the leaves and the surroundings. Arjuna, however, replies saying that he is only able to see the arrow and the bird's eye. The guru is highly pleased and recommends that everyone follow Arjuna's example. This tale has been told to us from childhood to teach us the importance of focus.

We can take inspiration from this story to discuss focus and its physiology, and the tools that can help us improve it. The basics of focus are tied to neurobiology and our understanding of the brain. We discussed the old and new brain earlier; while emotions and memories are stored and controlled by the older part of the brain, the pre-frontal cortex, the new brain, controls focus and awareness.

When you focus, you train the brain to selectively activate only relevant neurons so that the noise of extra information gets discarded and we process only the selected data. In our default unfocused state, our attention is spread wide. Imagine the brain as a dartboard of neurons. When we focus, we throw a dart and hit the bullseye. When we lose focus, the dart changes into a hammer and, instead of hitting a particular, relevant set of neurons, we end up activating a lot of other unrelated neurons and create cognitive noise. The change of the dart to the hammer activates other neurons with various functions, and we start receiving and processing a lot of extra information that we might not need. Focusing is the continuous exercise of bringing back and sharpening the arrow whenever it starts changing into a hammer. Many interventions can aid us in this process of improving focus.

The first step is to understand our *ultradian rhythm*. In the 1950s, Nathaniel Kleitman, during his research on sleep patterns, discovered that the human body tends to move through some cycles of high and low energy levels during the day. These cycles, where we experience different energy levels and alertness, are called ultradian cycles and typically last about ninety minutes. Jim Loehr, in his book *The Power of Full Engagement*, writes,

These ultradian rhythms help to account for the ebb and flow of our energy throughout the day. Physiological measures such as heart rate, hormonal levels, muscle tension, and brain-wave activity all increase during the first part of the cycle—and so does alertness. After an hour or so, these measures start to decline. Somewhere between 90 and 120 minutes, the body begins to crave a period of rest and recovery.

Ultradian Performance Rhythm

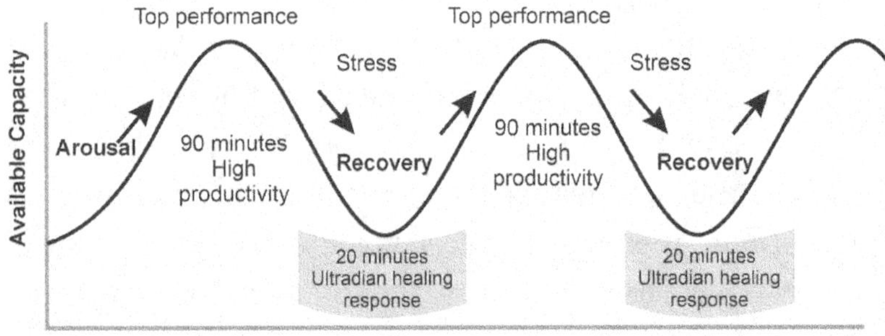

If we are in sync with our ultradian rhythms, we can slot high-focus and high-intensity work when the rhythm swings upward for about ninety minutes, and then rest and defocus during the ebb. Proper rest in the form of digital detox and complete wiring down of the neurons is essential. The sharper the focus, the more you need to rest. In fact, during the rest period, you need to practise deliberate defocusing. Whatever your chosen activity, completely move away from digital screens and work.

Another quick behaviour fix to improve focus is adding music to the preparation ritual. The entire cycle of the brain trying to come into focus mode takes the brain ten to fifteen minutes. A study published in the journal *Frontiers in Human Neuroscience* found that participants who listened to 40 Hz binaural beats showcased increased levels of focus on demanding cognitive tasks.[9] A binaural beat is an auditory illusion in which slightly different frequencies are played in each ear, which leads

---

9   '5 Amazing Benefits of 40-Hz Binaural Beats', *Voise Foundation*, 30 November 2023, https://www.voisefoundation.org/5-amazing-benefits-of-40-hz-binaural-beats/.

to a synchronised brainwave formation that induces a state of focus. For example, if you play a beat of 200 Hz in your left ear and 210 Hz in your right ear, the binaural beat will be 10 Hz, which is the difference between the frequency of the two beats. Imagine Amitabh speaking in one ear and SRK in the other; you are bound to focus naturally to make sense of anything. YouTube has many channels with such beats; play any that catches your fancy for five minutes before you start your focused work; 40 Hz beats have been proven to be the most effective in increasing focus. This practice will have two benefits: one, it will begin signalling to your brain that you are now getting into focus mode, and second, the brain will start releasing the necessary chemicals to sharpen the arrow of focus.

Focus is also affected by our diet—what and how much we eat matters. The brain is the most energy-hungry organ in the human body—to maintain voluntary and involuntary activities, brain cells or neurons pass electric charges to communicate with each other. As I type this sentence, my brain neurons are passing an electric charge, similar to a computer binary code, instructing my fingers to move on the keyboard. The brain needs energy to maintain this charge exchange between the neurons. Like all kids and many Indian adults, neurons love sweets (glucose).

Food and neurons have a complex relationship. When you are fasting, your body has less glucose in the blood. We must have mentioned many a time that we cannot focus on anything when we are hungry. The entire campaign of the candy bar Snickers is based on how we can't even identify with our regular selves when hungry. So, being too low in glucose disagrees with neurons, and they cannot be appropriately activated. High levels of glucose doesn't work either. If you eat a sumptuous, oily meal, the brain has to send all the blood to the digestive system to digest the food. Hence, there is less for the hungry brain, and we start feeling sleepy.

If we observe these critical patterns of our bodies, we should be able to address our focus needs through our food habits.

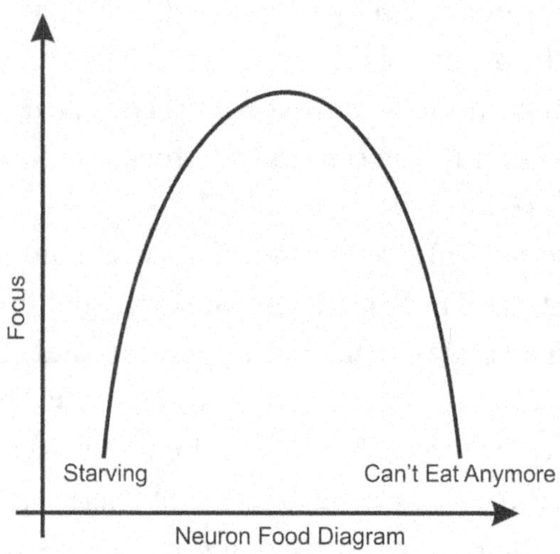

Along with food, caffeine also has significant effects on our focus. Caffeine increases the production of dopamine and adrenalin, hormones that drive focus. But it also leads to difficulties in sleeping if taken too late. It is an experiment we all have to do with our bodies, such as how much caffeine we can take and when we should stop so that it doesn't affect sleep. The ideal recommended dosage is to only have coffee two hours after waking up and stop seven to eight hours before your usual time to sleep.

Stress in healthy amounts also sharpens the arrow of focus as it increases adrenalin. One method that is becoming popular these days is giving cold exposure to our bodies. While the people doing it strongly recommend ice baths, this is not for the faint of heart. I have my own variation of cold exposure. After a hot shower, an excellent way to give some cold exposure to the body is by turning the shower knob the other way to cold. As it is, most Indian showers have just two settings: the scaldingly hot lava of Mordor on one side and a freezingly cold Arctic sea on the other. Drench yourself with cold water for as long as you can manage. Start small and do it only for five seconds, and try and increase it to thirty to sixty seconds. The effect on the body of this cold exposure is instantaneous.

A significant aspect of these experiments is that we can layer them and find the method that suits us best. We can also space them out and keep getting boosts of focus and Bright Energy throughout the day. If you plan a session of deep, focused work, start with a ritual of taking a cold shower, putting in some 40 Hz binaural beats and getting the focus hormones flooding your brain. After an hour or so, take a short break, go for a walk or prepare your coffee.

Come back and restart your focus work session, drinking caffeine to bring back the focus hormones while the 40 hz beats play in the background. This routine should help you deliver two sessions of deep, focused work of ninety minutes each. As suggested by Cal Newport in his book *Deep*

Work, a healthy human mind cannot do more than four hours of deep work in a day. But the amount and quality of work you would do in these four hours will be much better than eight or ten hours of shallow and unfocused work. In a day, having two or three such sessions can help you use your time best, delivering output with the sharpest focus and the highest and Brightest Energy.

Famous American neuroscientist and Stanford University professor Dr Andrew Huberman recommends an ancient Chinese meditation style as a quick exercise to improve focus. We have all seen movies like *The 36 Chambers of Shaolin*, where the hero wants to master kung fu, and his teacher orders him to spend seemingly unending days focusing on the flame of a candle. This story presents a deep-rooted scientific fact about the relationship between focus, cognition and vision. It wouldn't be incorrect to say that vision is the first step towards cognition and focus. That is why the vision-related circuitry occupies our brain's most extensive real estate.

How does the Shaolin chamber monk benefit from staring at the candle's flame? He is teaching his brain to reduce visual noise by focusing on a small area. He forms the neural networks and then makes them stronger by repeating this action for an extended period. This method of training is called *overt focusing*. To improve your overt focus, you need just one straightforward thing: it is easy, and you can do it anytime, at home, at the office, while travelling, waiting for your coffee or whenever you have idle thirty seconds. All you need is a point to direct your focus. In a preferably nonelectronic medium, choose a point. You may draw a simple cross on a Post-It and put it on your laptop screen to start the exercise. Just select one sharp point and start focusing while maintaining your breath. Let your breath and your focused attention on the selected point be the only things you can perceive. With practice, you will be able to drown out all the other noise of the surroundings.

This experience is the same as Arjuna and his bird's eye. Focus on something as small and sharp as the eye. Start with fifteen seconds and increase to one or two minutes. Doing this for more than two to three minutes will be difficult but not even required. Even after thirty seconds, people have reported a sharper focus increase. Do this exercise just before you start your deep, focused work block of the day and experiment with the results.

Another way to improve focus in a similar setting would be to do the diametrically opposite, the *covert focus technique*. This technique is a bit more challenging, so doing it even for thirty seconds should be enough. Take the same cross-marked paper and put it in your field of vision. But this time, try and focus on your peripheral vision. What do the most extreme left and right corners of your eyes see? Try to notice all you can see in your peripheral vision for as long as possible without moving your pupils.

You can perform all the exercises and experiments explained above separately or combined, multiple times during the day, to keep sustaining and improving your focus. It is natural and human to lose focus, but having the awareness to bring back the attention to your intended point of focus is what matters. That is the muscle we have to build. The arrow of focus will keep broadening to become a blunt hammer, but through these exercises and ramping up the chemicals that improve focus, we need to keep trying to sharpen the arrow to look only at the eye of the bird.

With an improvement in focus, you increase the intentional usage of time. Thus your relationship with time improves, and you are able to derive the most out of the time you have. Add the layer of Bright Energy to this, and if your focus is the sharpest when your Bright Energy is at its peak, your productivity will be at the highest for the time you can sustain this.

Bright Experiment: Focus Partners

While you can do this experiment standalone too, it works best if you team up with a friend or colleague and time each other for thirty-minute intervals.

They note everytime you lose focus and check your phone, email or give in to any other distraction, in the format below.

	The act of distraction	Emotion you felt	Internal/ external trigger	Focus duration (minutes)	Strategy to combat
1	Checked my phone while working on a report	Tired, bored	Internal	10	Try combatting it with binaural beats and caffeine
2	Checked a message on MS Teams	Irritated	External	15	Mute Teams during the focus hour

This should help you understand your focus patterns. Add various elements discussed above and notice if they aid in increasing the focus duration.

1.   40 Hz binaural beat: Focus Duration____________________

2.   Overt focusing: Focus Duration____________________

3.   Covert focusing: Focus Duration____________________

4.   Caffeine therapy: Focus Duration____________________

Experiment and see what works for you.

On our journey to improve our relationship with time, we have explored the waters of finding our purpose, making a plan for time on multiple scales, from a few years to our next birthday, and brought it closer to a weekly and daily plan. We have explored experiments to understand our Bright and Dark Energy reserves and how they affect the intentional usage of our time. We have understood the reasons for procrastination and how to overcome them. We have learnt techniques to prioritise effectively and sharpen our focus to make the best productive use of our time.

In the next section, let's see how we can apply all these experiences to the Indian workplace. What is the Indian workplace like, what happens in them and why, and how it leads to us wasting time. What can we each do in our limited circles of influence to ensure we spend our time effectively and can do away with this constant overwhelming feeling we have whenever we think of work?

In the next section, we will try to find tools to help us stop hating Mondays.

- Bright work = Time spent x Focus x Bright Energy
- Focus is an important element in our relationship with time.
- Reasons behind losing focus:
  - Lack of planning and hence having no awareness of what to focus on
  - Volatile emotions that override our cognitive direction
  - Attention residue from previous tasks
  - Too many or too few breaks in our work schedule
  - Lack of sleep and Bright Energy recharging
- When you focus, you train the brain to selectively activate only relevant neurons, to discard the noise and process only selected data.
- Ultradian rhythm: The human body moves through cycles of ninety minutes of high and low energy, with alternating period of top performance and recovery. Understand your ultradian rhythm and slot high-focus activities to coincide with the top-performance swing of the curve.
- 40 Hz binaural beats help increase levels of focus.
- Food absorption causes fluctuations of glucose levels in the brain, and affects our ability to focus.
- Caffeine boosts focus, as it drives up the production of hormones that drive focus.
- Cold exposure releases copious amounts of focus hormones.

- Layering of all these focusing techniques can give us a sustained focus trajectory over the entire day.
- To be more focused is to be more intentional with our time and to derive the best out of what we have.

Section 3

Time at the Workplace

Chapter 11

Our Poor Relation with Time

For no fault of its own, Monday is the most despised day the world over. The gloom of Monday dread starts kicking from the late evening hours of Sunday itself; such is its terror. Why do you think that is the case?

I believe it is the lack of power to choose how we want to spend our time that causes us to dread Mondays. Over the weekend, we typically have more control over what we do. So, unless you have unwanted relatives dropping in, some distant cousin's wedding to attend or a tiresome school event, you have a large chunk of time in which you get to decide what you want to do. You may spend that time watching Netflix or cricket, sleeping or engaging in a hobby you like, but the choice is yours.

We miss this control over the time we spend at the office. From the time of entry, when you punch in your attendance, till you leave the office, which can vary depending on how the day goes, this lack of control over your time makes us uncomfortable. We are nothing but the time we have. Since we spend most of our weekday waking hours at the office, we feel we are wasting our life force with control in someone else's hands.

In a high context and collective culture like India, this takes an even uglier turn. In our culture, we are expected to respect the manager so much that even if we have no significant work, we feel ashamed to return home if they are still in the office. Hierarchy is an important driver of our behaviours. Indian managers have far more overt and covert control over their employee's time than in the West. As many of us complain, in India, while the punch-in time is fixed, punch-out depends on the boss. Hierarchy shapes how we approach deadlines, punctuality and our attitude towards time.

People pleasing, sacrificing your comfort for the greater collective good, deferring to and respecting elders are cultural values deeply ingrained in all of us. At the workplace, this respect for authority translates to us dancing forever to the boss's tune. We attempt to rise to their expectations, seldom negotiate the timelines they set and change our workday priorities at any request or suggestion from them. The seeming obligation to meet the demands of the management keeps us on our toes, and we see our workday routine frequently disrupted to keep up with prompt closures of these demands.

Fear of repercussions for failing to comply with these demands runs deep too. As managers hold considerable control over career trajectories, pleasing and keeping them happy is a natural desire for anyone looking to grow. The manager holds the cards of how much money we make and the kind of lifestyle we have, so we feel we can't be bold and assertive. The long and short of it is that as employees, especially at the junior levels, we have minimal control of our time during the workday and heavily depend on the company's culture and the manager we work for.

Busyness and 'Pseudo-productivity'

Another added cultural nuance is the concept of busyness. When we were an agricultural economy, the longer you worked in the field, the higher your output; hence, time spent was a clear indicator of productivity. With industrialisation, the same metric continued—the more time one spent on the assembly line, the more units one could produce. However, when we moved to a knowledge economy, we did not necessarily shift our concept of productivity. With the advent of the service industry and call centres, IT and ITeS companies carried forward the traditional definitions of productivity. Unlike an assembly line or a field, the output of a knowledge worker is not necessarily immediately tangible. This work happens often through thinking, conversations and collaboration, and depends on multiple other people performing together. For most knowledge work jobs, we can't quantify daily or hourly the number of knowledge units a person worked upon. For this reason, the metric of time spent in the office continues to be used as a crutch to define productivity.

This erratic and archaic definition of productivity is at the centre of all that is wrong with our relationship with time at the workplace. We track and reward this pseudo productivity; hence, employees are forced to project that they are spending time in the office, espousing and encouraging a culture where busyness means productivity.

If you spend upwards of ten or twelve hours in the office, even if you aren't doing any actual high-quality work or are fully engrossed in endless meetings for this duration, the system is designed to see this busyness as a measure of productivity, and more often than not will reward you. In India, it is not smart work, not even hard work; it is *long work* that gets significant recognition.

The problem with long work and busyness is that it diminishes the output and fills us with Dark Energy, further deteriorating the quality of work. It compels you to be outwardly busy, which is a huge drain on your energy. Hence, your output is Dark Matter. Long work means losing control on your time, and that adds to the Dark Energy pool too. Any work output that you give under compulsion, feeling as if you don't control your time, will likely be suboptimal and Dark.

Another frequently seen behaviour in the Indian workspace is the level of urgency for every single task. Everything was needed yesterday. People share half-baked briefs with huge buffers of time built in, leading to long working hours for teams responsible for delivering them. This is followed by multiple iterations, as the approvers and doers try to churn out a decent output. Multiple reworks, last-minute urgent changes and iterations in the brief itself moments before delivery are commonplace. This lack of planning reflects a deeper lack of empathy about others' time and comfort—money is being paid, so work will be demanded. We love to extract more than our money's worth to feel a sense of our resources being spent well. A default expectation that employees will put in long working hours and late nights to deliver last-minute requests is commonplace.

Indian corporate employees struggle with various time sinks. These are Dark Energy pools that exacerbate negative time-related behaviours:

- *Endless meetings without clear agendas*: We are in a constant review cycle, a system resembling Russian nesting dolls. Juniors have to sit for a review to prepare for a review that the manager will take because her manager has to prepare for a review. Clear agendas are lacking, so there is no clear decision output, and the cycle continues. Sending mass email invites to all and sundry is another time sink. You have to attend the entire sixty-minute meeting for a potential participation of mere two minutes.
- *Bureaucratic delays*: Given the multiple layers and mistrust in management on lower-rung employees, decision-making is more or less centralised. This leads to bureaucratic inaction with several levels of approvals needed for even minor decisions. Even in this digital age, India is a high experience culture and we prefer in-person discussions instead of faster digital approvals.
- *Reliance on jugaad*: Jugaad is the quintessential Indian standard operating procedure, or SOP, to get things done in the workplace. Given most of the workplaces do not have set SOPs in place or some are so tiresome that employees are forced to find shortcuts to get their work done. These jugaad workarounds create more long-term problems than solving for root causes. The

jugaad approach leads to duplicate, sub-standard work that takes a lot more of the employees' time compared to following a systemic approach.

- *Unclear job roles*: The hustle culture of Indian start-ups has a lot of pros, but it is a time management nightmare, with its 'everyone does everything' approach. There are no defined roles, and multitasking is the rule. Multitasking leads to massive inefficiency. The whole start-up ecosystem can benefit immensely if it can implement 'intelligent hustle'—hustle like crazy, but only after setting clear boundaries of time and roles so that employees do deep work and not waste time getting constantly distracted by shallow, non-value-adding tasks.

Bright Exercise: The Busyness Audit

Go through your calendar of last two weeks and continue this exercise for the next two weeks.

Divide the workday into six sections:

1. Bright Work (deep focused work, productive meetings with clear a agenda and outcomes)

2. Dark Work (unproductive shallow tasks, unnecessary meetings without a clear agenda)

3. Administrative work (expenses filing, report filing, attendance, reply to emails, etc.)

4. Breaks (were they to unwind and refresh or gossip and distract?)

5. Multitasking incidents (how many task switches did you do in a day?)

6.   Unwanted interruptions (how often and for what duration were you pulled into something other than what you were working on?)

Give yourself a daily 'busyness score'. The lower the score, the better your professional life:

Busyness Score = (Dark Work + Administrative Work + Distracting Breaks + Multitasks + Interruptions) / (Bright Work + Refresh Breaks)

If you stay in the office for eight hours and do four hours of Bright Work with sixty minutes of scattered refreshing breaks, and do administrative work for the other three hours, your busyness score would be:

$$\text{Busyness score} = 3/5 = 0.6$$

Given that the human mind cannot do more than four hours of deep, focused bright work, this is the lowest busyness score value: 0.6. The closer your score is to 0.6, the better are you using your time at the workplace.

If your busyness score is greater than 1, it means you are spending more time doing Dark Work and need to review your to-do lists.

Infrastructure Issues

We discussed how our collectivist cultural roots and poor relationship with time create a problem of time availability at the workplace. By rewarding busyness and long work, Indian corporates are driving negative time-related behaviours in its employees. But that is just a part of the problem. Employees are not only wasting time looking busy and working idle long hours but they are also wasting a lot of time in commuting.

This becomes the final nail in the problem of time availability at the Indian workplace—the overall lack of infrastructure in Indian metros. Be it Bangalore, Mumbai, Pune or the National Capital Region, traffic jams are the norm at rush hour. On bad days, people spend around two hours travelling to and from the office. When about three or four hours of your waking day are spent just in travel, time suddenly becomes very scarce. This travel cuts short the day from being twenty-four hours to just twenty. With this strain on available time, we need to consider optimising even the travel time to be more intentional.

Given these cultural and socio-economic factors, knowledge workers in India are already operating at a significant disadvantage concerning time available compared to their counterparts in the West. Hence, there are complaints of deep exhaustion, burnout and a mentality to escape the current manager or company and land in a new but similar situation in a different company.

Even with this reality of the Indian workspace, all is not lost. With some initiative, drive and tact, we can still gain a modicum of control over our time within our limited circle of influence. While all the experiments and recommendations we studied above can be implemented at the workplace, something more fundamental needs to be addressed before we start implementing them.

- The greatest source of anxiety and discomfort at the workplace is not having control over how we spend our time.
- Negative time-related behaviours are perpetuated by our collectivist culture that demands deference to seniors and sacrificing the comfort of the individual for the greater good.
- Managers hold significant control over career trajectories of employees, and hence deference to them is significant, especially at junior levels.
- The Indian workplace rewards not smart work, not even hard work, but long work. The common assumption is that the longer you are in the office, the more productive and loyal you are.
- Showing you are 'busy' is often more important than delivering quality work. Indian managers reward busyness as it is easy to track.
- Other time sinks that gnaw away the time available to employees include:
  - Endless meetings without a clear agenda
  - Bureaucratic delays
  - Reliance on jugaad
  - Unclear job roles
- Poor infrastructure, drowning under the massively growing Indian population, is another reason

employees spend a significant portion of their productive time in commuting.
- Using mindfulness and time-saving strategies can help give some control back to the employee.

CHAPTER 12

Reclaiming Time at the Workplace

IMAGINE THE PREHISTORIC WORKPLACE. CAVEPEOPLE Rahul, Anjali, Prem and Nisha are hungry and want to hunt some deer. Deer are incredibly agile and difficult to catch, and our team has just sticks and stones to attack and capture their prey. Any hope for success depends heavily on their coordination, and they have developed their own language to do that. Some hoots help direct everyone towards the target, and some mock bird calls help them triangulate its position. Everyone is focused, alert and fully committed to succeeding in this one task, as they will go hungry otherwise.

This sequence is how people collaborated and communicated while at work in prehistoric times. Not much changed in workplace communication as the eras passed and humans evolved from being hunters to farmers. Only communication technologies developed: people used letters and runners to engage with people beyond the reach of their voices. With industrialisation, machines and trains, communication time shrank, and with the advent of the telephone, it became almost instantaneous. It became possible for a hunter in Mumbai to call a hunter in Delhi and plan hunts for deer together.

But one thing changed. The mind of the caveperson was highly trained to work with focus on only one task at a time. Not so in the modern world. Imagine Rahul in Delhi, gathering some berries, his mind entirely focused on the bush in front of him. He is so focused that he is picking ten berries per minute. He gets a call from Anjali in Mumbai, and she starts talking about her hunting plan. She has bought a nice spear from Mogambo & Co. Rahul humours her for some time and then disconnects. His mind, which was so engrossed in berry picking, now has some images of deer hunting and a shiny new spear running through it. His attention gets divided, and his berry-picking rate drops to barely six berries per minute.

Further evolution happened, and Rahul and Anjali entered the 1990s, and got introduced to a revolutionary tool, the email. At any point, without any significant cost, they could communicate their ideas, share photos of their new hunting tools, negotiate purchases of new berry gathering equipment and discuss plans for when they wanted to go on an expedition. To add to their convenience, around 2010, they got a handheld smartphone that made email, calls and messaging instantaneous and constantly available.

Today, with the technology and new shiny tools available, his management is able to grow far more berries and expects Rahul to gather much more than ten berries per minute. Rahul reaches his allocated place and starts picking berries. He starts getting WhatsApp messages from Anjali, who wants him to stop gathering berries and go on a hunt instead. Rahul also starts getting multiple emails from Prem, who wants him to come and repair his old berry gathering machine. Nisha, his manager, is asking for reports on how many he plans to gather this month and demanding reasons for why his berry picking was so lacklustre last week. He is also getting frantic calls from an angry customer to whom he delivered rotten berries. With so many pings of messages and calls, his mind keeps switching contexts from one activity to the next. There is so much work, so many messages to read and respond to, so many approvals to take, so many fights to fight and so little time—how can he do it all? He breaks down, there is a huge surge in his Dark Energy and his berry-picking rate goes to zero.

This story is an attempt to illustrate how the evolution of technology is not necessarily a step towards improved productivity and better time usage at the workplace. We are in no position to say that with all the tools available today, we are being more productive and working with far greater focus than we were earlier. Our mind has become what the Buddhists call the monkey mind. We jump from one idea and thought to another instantly, and our mind buzzes with the overload of information and sensations we get from our surroundings. We are absorbing everything and retaining nothing.

When we were cave dwellers and single-tasking, our Bright Energy levels were decent, and with limited distractions we finished our work to the best of our abilities. Now, with so many energy-sapping tools like email and WhatsApp , we get distracted easily and our Bright Energy reserves fall further in every attempt we make to refocus. The overload of information also confuses us and leads to an increase in our anxiety and Dark Energy.

With this reality facing us at work, how do we reclaim time? How do we manage our Bright Energy? How do we deliver the best that we have the potential to deliver? How do we sharpen our focus to do our best work? How do we align our goals with our manager's so that there are no unwanted interruptions and Dark Energy-raising tasks?

The key to bringing any change is to solve two interconnected problems: communication and attention. Let's explore some strategies for these.

Communication Strategies

Being able to communicate properly is the key to making our lives a little easier at work. And this begins with having a clear conversation with your manager. Below are some strategies to navigate this smoothly.

Strategy #1: Prepare thoroughly

- Before the meeting with your manager, list all your to-dos and put them in the Eisenhower prioritisation matrix based on your understanding.

- Keep your weekly work plan ready, with your Bright Stars for each day of the following week mentioned clearly.
- Make a list of potential issues and possible solutions. While no one likes to hear problems, it is usually an excellent strategy to go prepared with recommended solutions. Suggest priorities and timelines from your perspective.

Strategy #2: Schedule a meeting

- Schedule a formal meeting with a specific agenda to discuss your workload and your recommendations on priorities and timelines.
- This clarity ensures that this agenda is given the proper attention it deserves and is not clubbed or rushed in the middle of other agendas.

Strategy #3: Present your Eisenhower matrix

- Discuss the priorities and timelines you have set and ask for your manager's recommendations on edits.
- As superiors, managers have access to more information than you and can help you reprioritise or even completely revamp your prioritisation matrix.
- However, once you set the priorities in the matrix along with negotiated and agreed possible timelines, the manager becomes acutely aware of all the tasks in your tray and how you have planned to execute them.
- Initially, set these priorities for a more manageable time horizon, like a week and not a month.

Strategy #4: Express commitment

- Once the priority matrix and timelines are set and discussed, express complete commitment from your side to deliver within these timelines.
- Build trust with the manager by delivering tasks within the agreed timelines or keep them updated in case there is any deviation. Most of the issues at work arise because employees don't communicate delays or issues in time.

Strategy #5: Make it publicly accessible

- Publicly declare and showcase your Eisenhower matrix to your manager and peers to let them know what pieces you are working on and when.
- This declaration helps everyone know what you are working on, and they will recalibrate their expectations from you based on the workload they can see.

This simple exercise, when done for six to eight weeks with your manager before the start of the work week, can help you significantly reduce the overflow of work and allow you some control over your time. With time, trust builds, and maintaining a clear and publicly declared set of priorities can help the entire team plan the group's work with a shared vision. Clear communication brings empathy.

Meetings Galore

Another derailer of productivity at the workplace is the plethora of meetings we all have to attend. At the Indian corporate we are plagued with back-to-back, unending meetings that can last even the whole day, in some cases. For some of us, the work day can look like this on left, or this on the right.

10	M1
	M2
11	M3
	M4
12	M5
	M6
1	LUNCH
2	M7
	M8
3	M9
	M10
4	M11
	M12
5	M13
	M14
6	M15

10	M1
11	
12	
1	LUNCH
2	M2
3	
4	
5	
6	

Both kinds of workdays have their own challenges. In the first one, where we have back-to-back meetings, we are hit heavily by the attention residue effect. While attending Meeting 4, your mind might still be mulling over all the information you received in M3, M2 and M1. Hence, your contribution to M4 will be subpar.

An intelligent method, derived from the Pomodoro technique, to break this attention residue chain is to take five-minute breaks between the meetings. Start scheduling meetings for twenty-five minutes instead of thirty or fifty-five minutes instead of sixty. That leaves five minutes for you to unwind before you tackle the next problem. During this short break, take a walk, chat with some colleagues, call your family, listen to your favourite song or unwind in any way that takes you away from your laptop/mobile screens. You can also add a ritual after every meeting to summarise the meeting in one or two lines, writing it down on a piece of paper or your laptop. It helps kick off the Zeigarnik effect discussed earlier and tricks your mind into releasing the information gathered in its RAM (pre-frontal cortex) as the task seems complete.

Jeff Bezos and the folks at Amazon have found an innovative way to deal with the time sink of meetings. They have completely done away with PowerPoint presentations and have moved to paper and memos. This practice addresses an often-overlooked aspect: the content and agenda of the meeting itself. How often have we all commented, 'This meeting could have been an email!' We are all pulled into loosely run meetings with no proper agenda, pre-decided outcome or expected decision. This behaviour is rampant in the Indian workplace. While meeting culture and outcomes are primarily driven top-down, we can at least start striving for some change in our limited circle of influence. The next time you get a meeting invite with the title 'discussion' or anything vague, your Dark Energy signals should go up! You should politely, maybe one-on-one, push the meeting organiser to share two pieces of information: first, the agenda or the flow of the meeting recommended, and second, the critical decisions or outcomes expected. Sharing pre-reads and memos can also be an excellent way to ensure people are prepared for the meeting.

Good Meeting Flow

- Start with the why
  - Explain the objective of the meeting clearly, before the meeting begins, preferably in the invite itself.
  - Define and share a list of topics and specify the sequence in the agenda and the decisions or outcomes expected for each topic listed.
- Timeboxing
  - Specify a precise time slot for each topic discussion. Stick to these timeboxes to avoid the discussions dragging unnecessarily.
  - Use visual or audio aides to see the time lapsed and keep sharpening the discussion within the allotted time. Set timers that beep and indicate the end of a slot, forcing the attendees to wrap up a topic.
  - Limit the overall length of the meeting to short bouts of thirty or at most sixty minutes to prevent fatigue. A better time slot will be twenty-five or fifty-five minutes to give the last five minutes for unwinding and relaxing before the next meeting.
- Assign roles
  - Facilitator, time-keeper, note-taker, devil's advocate—assign these roles to people to ensure the meetings don't end up in chaos and the best, fully rounded decisions emerge.

- Bias for closure
  - Stay on topic; the facilitator's job is to keep bringing the meeting back to the topic being discussed within the time allotted.
  - Create a 'parking space', a blank whiteboard space where you park the ideas or topics that crop up as side issues to the discussed topic. These ideas or issues can be set aside to speak about at later meetings, and the discussion can be brought back to the issue at hand without the fear of losing an important point.
  - At the end of the meeting, recap the key decisions and outcomes achieved for each topic and review the next steps and clear responsibilities for timelines and actions to be taken, before everyone leaves the meeting.
  - To ensure everyone is on the same page, send the minutes of the meeting summarising what decisions were made and what the next steps are.

Here is an example of two-hour meetings, starting at 10 a.m.

Time Slot	Agenda Item	Presenter	Decision to be Taken
10.00–10.05	Context Setting	Meeting Organiser	Confirm attendance and objectives.
10.05–10.30	Project Updates	Team Lead	Agree on project status and next steps.

10.30– 10.55	Discussion on Challenges	Team Member 1	Identify key challenges and potential solutions.
10.55– 11.00	Break		
11.00– 11.20	Strategy planning	Department Head	Decide on strategic priorities and allocation of resources.
11.20– 11.40	Q&A and Open Discussion	All Participants	Gather feedback and additional concerns.
11.40– 11.50	Action Items Review	Meeting Organiser	Confirm action items and responsible parties.
11.50– 11.55	Closing Remarks	Meeting Organiscr	Ensure clarity on next meeting date and follow-up.
11.55– 12.00	Break		

If we have any hope of reclaiming our time in the workplace, the first step is to address the culture of the company or our team around meetings. Otherwise, we will always be pulled into these endless time-guzzling vertices and will never find time to do any focused work.

Escape the Email Dark Matter

How often have we all felt depressed looking at the sheer quantum of emails staring at us in our inbox? Email, a miraculous innovation that revolutionised communication, has now become one of the biggest hindrances to employee happiness, productivity and collaboration. Exhaustion by email is a reality and pretty commonplace. Email is one of the biggest Dark Energy creators in the workplace. To reclaim our time, we must decode the email problem and understand how to engage better with this tool.

Research suggests that an average employee checks their email once every five minutes, and a third of them check it every three minutes.[10] This is a significant drain on focus. Email is precisely the trigger our monkey mind needs to keep jumping on the next shiny thing and never finish whatever it was working on.

When the monkey mind engages with email, it creates Dark Energy. Let's say you and I are involved in one project. To close that project successfully, we have to send emails to each other. Let's assume we send ten back-and-forth emails each day. This scenario is manageable as we can continue our focused work and easily check and reply to ten emails. The reality is we are all working on about ten different projects of various levels of urgency with different people. You have to prepare a report, approve a work order, review a submission, interview a new candidate, give feedback to a team member, schedule an important meeting and so on.

Through a simple extension of logic, these ten back-and-forth emails for ten projects will lead to a hundred back-and-forth emails. This level is where the system starts to

---

10   Maxi Heitmayer and Saadi Lahlou, 'Why Are Smartphones Disruptive? An Empirical Study of Smartphone Use in Real-Life Contexts', *Computers in Human Behavior*, 116, March 2021, https://www.sciencedirect.com/science/article/abs/pii/S0747563220303848.

break down. As discussed in previous sections, it takes the brain twelve to fifteen minutes to get into focus mode and harness our Bright Energy to deliver results. However, with the many emails that need attention, we are forced to keep shifting our context every few minutes.

Let's say you are trying to prepare a report that requires deep-work for three hours. About fifteen minutes in, you get an email asking to approve a work order. Now, the ping of email breaks your concentration.

Research by the University of Berkeley shows that receiving new emails in anticipation of new information releases the same reward hormone, dopamine, that we get when we eat our favourite food, earn money or win prizes.[11] The craving for that reward hormone drives the monkey mind to jump towards the next shiny thing, which, in this case, is the new information that this incoming email might have. The content of the email is immaterial; our brain is trained to crave the reward of opening the email itself.

Our monkey mind is now so addicted to this reward hormone that we crave its release, and hence are unable to concentrate on the report. Instead, we keep checking our email to see if we have any new shiny objects to play with. As suggested by the research, the statistic of one look at our phone every five minutes sounds entirely plausible. But this is not where the problem ends. We got an email, we got the dopamine reward and we approved the work order that the email requested of

---

11   'Your Brain Gets a Dopamine Hit from Information', *Neuroscience News & Research*, 20 June 2019, https://www.technologynetworks. com/neuroscience/news/your-brain-gets-a-dopamine-hit-from-information-320878.

us. But now, when we go back to our main task of preparing the report, it will take us another twelve to fifteen minutes to get into Bright focus mode. This phenomenon is called context switching. This switching of contexts and the related loss in focus, Bright Energy and thereby productivity is where emails and messages hurt the most.

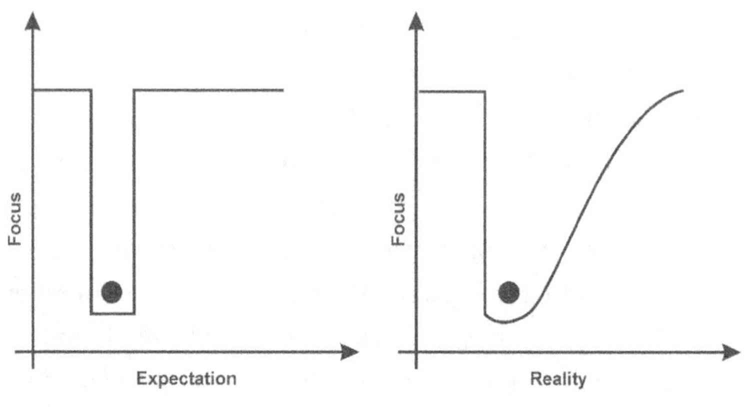

Let's look at a reel quickly

This context switching puts an enormous cognitive load on our brains. Imagine switching the context for a hundred back-and-forth emails; it is like juggling a hundred balls at once or trying to remember multiple movie plot lines together. The diagram above is an approximation of how email interruptions affect your focus. After addressing the interruption, we expect to bounce back instantaneously to the original level of focus, Bright Energy and effectiveness. But the reality is far removed from that, eventually leading to a complete loss of focus and even, in severe cases, a complete loss of motivation to continue working.

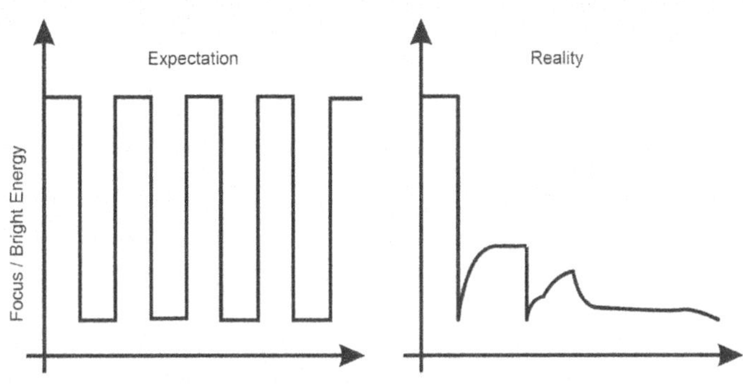

Effect on focus of reading multiple emails

The cost of context shifting is immense; we pay for it with our time and Bright Energy. Along with this context switching and the constant interruptions that lead us away from focused work, let's see some more effects and the costs of unregulated usage of email.

The Problems

1. *Decision fatigue*: Every email opens a can of decisions for us: whether to open it or not, whether to reply or not, if we have to answer, when should it be replied to, should we keep the email marked as unread or important so that we can refer to it later, should we delegate the work to someone else, or whether we should just delete or ignore it. In the few seconds after you receive the email, your monkey mind goes through these various mental hoops, and no matter how small, you are forced to make these decisions. Making these decisions for hundreds of emails daily contributes to decision fatigue. By the end of the day, your Bright

Energy batteries are drained, and even deciding what to watch on TV becomes irritating.

2. *Email wars*: We love challenges, and as thoroughbred Indians, we are also extremely sensitive. Any seemingly undue or mildly accusatory email that comes our way meets with the swiftest and strongest rebuttal. We have all thought, 'How dare he write to me like that, with twenty other people marked!' We quickly reply, and thence begins a tennis volley of back-and-forth rejoinders, complaints and blame game. The twenty people who have been CCed in the email are either enjoying the match, or cursing at being made to endure it, or just plain bewildered at the childishness of the whole thing while they, too, have been that child multiple times.

    Nevertheless, the more you respond, the more emails you receive, and the more replies and defences you need to make. This vicious cycle can spiral out of control, and a simple reply can become a lot more work and distraction, keeping you away from the actual work. This is all Dark Matter and is a big drain on time and possibly your reputation.

3. *Quick response expectations*: Try as we might establish boundaries, some team cultures expect, recognise and reward instant or quick email replies. An instant reply is expected, failing which the efficiency or even capability of the employee gets questioned. While there can be some emails that need lightning speed replies, the team culture may expect this swift response more as a rule than as an exception. If you have to cater to

this metric of timely response, maintaining focus and doing quality work has to take a back seat.

All these problems are valid for more than just email. Emails now have been substituted by WhatsApp messages, pings on MS Teams or notifications from other messaging platforms. Bosses' and employees' monkey minds are all busy playing with and juggling multiple interruptions demands for each other's attention and an unending game of ping-pong. The problem is not with email as a tool but with the way our work habits have evolved and with our default distracted mode.

In the area of knowledge work, responsibility and, to a great extent, autonomy seem to be given to the employee. The management provides people with slightly long-term objectives, maybe monthly or quarterly, and they are expected to figure out means to achieve those targets independently. It is a basic assumption that every employee should be able to figure out how to deliver those targets in the time agreed and plan their work schedules accordingly. If you aim to sell a hundred units in one hundred hours, it is ultimately your call—if you sell ninety-nine units in one hour or one unit per hour for the next one hundred hours, the choice and authority are deemed yours. This is the grand illusion we all live in.

We all rely on others for our targets and objectives. To make the sale, you are dependent on product understanding, government approvals, marketing tools, money to generate leads, pitch deck to make the pitch and so on. And you are dependent on multiple other people to get these tools and resources. You reach out to these folks, but they have a hundred other priorities of their own. The result is you end up sending email requests to these people, escalating it to more senior stakeholders as and when required, in the hope of them giving some share of their time to help you succeed, which might not in any way benefit them. Why will anyone? And so the cycle of email wars continues.

Bright Exercise: The Inbox Detox

Go through your email exchanges for today. Count and put numbers to the following:

T = Total emails received in your inbox

S = Emails you sent

Y = Emails you could have avoided replying to or sending, could have called or closed in person

Z = Emails you could have avoided receiving altogether (random CC emails)

Calculate:

Required inbox = R = T − Z

Required outbox = X = S − Y

Email Health = H = R / X

Ideally this should be as close to 1 as possible.

Actions:

1. Track the email health ratio weekly to see patterns and trends.

2. Put all the senders of Z in a separate 'Clutter' folder, then try and bring Z close to zero.

3. Try and bring Y close to zero.

The Solutions

If we want to break out of this vicious cycle, we first need to break the monkey mind behaviour. We have to bring about a fundamental change in the way we operate with our teams. Before we look at some strategies that will help us bring some change to this behaviour in our circles of influence, let's understand the various kinds of messaging or communication that happen in offices.

1. *The questions*: This is one of the most common forms of email shared across organisations. Requests for budget approvals, reviews, appointment availability, project go-ahead, understanding of project scope, follow-up on deadlines, etc., are all some of the questions that people constantly ask each other. These form the backbone of our work and must be adequately addressed.

2. *The conversations*: These are back-and-forth two-way or, at times, multi-person communication chains. Depending on the complexity of the issue, each conversation chain can go up to hundreds of emails. These are the biggest guzzlers of time and a significant drain on productivity.

3. *The broadcasts*: These are emails that need to be sent to multiple large groups of people to disseminate some vital or administrative information. 'The schedule for this month's engagement calendar' and 'The latest summer fashion is in stores now' are the kinds of emails that are usually broadcast.

4. *The administrative workload*: These are the kind of activities that do not add much value to work but need to be done to stick to SOPs and maintain a trail of actions and decisions. Filing for reimbursements, applying for leaves and benefits, approving these for the team members on portals, claiming travel and food bills, etc., are all necessary parts of the modern workday.

Bright Exercise: The Email Brightness Index (EBI)

For the last one week, go through your work emails, both received and sent, and count the four types of email exchanges:

a. Questions (Q): Where some direct or indirect action that created business value and a surge of Bright Energy in you.

b. All emails that are admin work (A), broadcasts (B) and conversations (C).

Your email brightess index is as follows: EBI = Q / (A+B+C)

The higher the EBI, the better you are managing email Dark Matter.

Now that we understand these broad categories of workplace communication, we can consider strategies to help us better manage our email exchanges and thence our time.

1. *Email batching*: One necessary step to carve out Bright Work blocks is to completely dissociate from any form of email or WhatsApp communication for a certain period, and then allocate a fixed slot to processing email and messages.

   Experiment with your ultradian rhythms, understand when your energy is the brightest and then arrive at the time blocks that work for you. Give the brightest energy slots to deep, focused work—your Bright Stars—while low energy blocks should be used to respond to emails. Pump up high-energy music or take a good shot of caffeine before you start the email processing block to continue the momentum and not get bored or get the Dark Energy levels to rise.

   Giving specific time blocks to email also trains your monkey mind not to crave an email every five minutes. When you know you have an upcoming email block, you can guide all the restlessness of the mind to that block. This behaviour allows you to focus on your work without interruptions and the cognitive load of multitasking.

2. *Avoid e-conversations*: As well established by research, there are better forms of communication than email. Much of the emotional truth is absent from the electronic medium; hence, many messages get

misinterpreted, and the communications keep getting lengthier and murkier. People should prefer a call or an in-person meeting to close conversations quickly. If you see an email conversation escalating, try to diffuse it by calling or arranging an in-person meeting.

3. *Prioritise and declutter*: Now that we know the four broad categories of workplace messaging, we should sort the emails into them and address them differently. Not every email needs the same kind of attention. Prioritise urgent messages from your manager and clients and deprioritise all admin and broadcast messages. Use filters and labels to organise your inbox. Like a clear working desk, an organised inbox can do wonders for your productivity and overall happiness while helping you focus on what truly matters.

4. *Batch admin and broadcasts*: The last two kinds of communication, admin work and broadcasts, can be clubbed together, with time carved out once or twice a week to finish these seemingly unimportant but necessary tasks. That way, you can educate everyone in your circles of influence to expect admin approvals at a particular time in the week, and they can plan accordingly. Whenever a new email asks for your approval or you receive a message from HR to fill out a mandatory survey, you can safely guide your monkey mind to the pre-carved time block in the week to finish these tasks. You can use the same administrative time block to check all broadcast messages and see if anything is relevant.

5. *Establish and respect boundaries*: One of the problems with the modern workplace is that it is present everywhere. We are accessible 24x7, and anyone can reach us at any time, whether during office hours or beyond. People who work with other countries and different time zones are particularly affected by this issue. In this scenario, establishing boundaries between where work stops and where non-work life begins becomes vital. Protect your personal time and disconnect from the workplace to recharge and respect the limits set by your colleagues too.

With these strategies, you should be able to reclaim some time in the office and carve out time to work with focus and high Bright Energy. While email is one of the most significant tools, time guzzlers and focus destroyers in the workplace, let us also look at how, in many other ways, technology has both aided and made it difficult for us to reclaim time at work.

Technology to the Rescue

Every day, mobile phone developers recognise some core human needs and create an app that helps solve them. Making the most of our time and being more productive, efficient, collaborative and focused were all needs that were recognised, and we have many software tools and apps that can help us reclaim time at the workplace. However, integrating technology into our workflow and daily lives requires thoughtful selection and planning. We don't just want another app in the plethora of apps already on our phones to lie useless and eat storage space. Let us explore some simple, easy-to-follow steps to help you recapture time and be more intentional.

Break the Doom Loop

The first step is to declutter your mobile phone. Our phones are massive guzzlers of our time. While mobiles have brought us together in an unprecedented hyper-connected world, they have also enslaved us to the content being pushed on their screens. We are all stuck in a doom loop of compulsive and obsessive scrolling on social media.

Research suggests that an average person scrolls through 300 feet of content daily.[12] That is the height of the Statue of Liberty. Next time you think of exercise, I hope you won't consider the 300 feet worth of exercise your fingers get in the doom loop, when they are scrolling through reels! We need to change.

Just like crash diets have rarely worked for anyone, I will not recommend that, to change, you go back to the era of landline phones and delete all the apps and every cool, life-enhancing feature that this powerful device offers. But at the same time, we need to differentiate between life-enriching and time-guzzling, life-destroying features of the device. Decluttering your phone can significantly

---

12 ‘8 Danger Signs of Zombie Scrolling and How to Protect Yourself’, *Newport Institute*, https://www.newportinstitute.com/resources/mental-health/zombie_scrolling/.

shift how you spend your time. Here's a step-by-step guide on decluttering and focusing on what truly matters to us.

1. Conduct an app audit
   a. Review all the apps and write down when you last used them. Any app you haven't used in the past ninety days is redundant and should be deleted.
   b. Retain only apps that keep you connected and that you frequently use for productivity, life enrichment and essential services.

2. Organise your home screen
   a. Our home screen is the most frequently used. As explained in the previous chapters, research shows that we see it every five minutes on average. Therefore, it makes sense to have it clean and organised.
   b. Keep the home screen clutter-free. Removing all social media and entertainment apps from the home screen is a good strategy to introduce at least some friction to the start of doom-scrolling by making them difficult to access.
   c. Rearrange your home screen to show only the most essential and most used apps. Since emails drain our productive time, removing email apps from the home screen would be a good idea. A clean home screen with not more than three to four app widgets will ensure you limit the non-essential usage of your phone.

3. Manage notifications

a. Disable notifications. Completely stop all notifications from your phone. If possible, get a dual SIM or different phone so your family and near and dear ones can call you for emergencies, and turn off notifications for everything else.

b. Most phones come with a Do Not Disturb feature, which bars all attempts to connect calls and messages for a specific period, except for some preselected options. Use this strategy for ninety-minute stretches of deep work.

4. Set time limits

a. Our phones have an inherent feature that tracks how much time we spend on our screens. Whatever gets tracked gets driven. Track where you spend your screen time. This information will be a good input to change app usage.

b. Set prescribed time limits for usage. Smartphones, both Android and Apple, support setting a time limit for app usage, after which it automatically shuts down. These limits can help take some control out of your hands to ensure you don't overindulge in Dark Matter or time-wasting apps like social media and video games.

c. Use apps like 'One Sec' to give you enough time to rethink when you accidentally and habitually click on the icon for a social media app. By giving yourself a few moments to take a deep breath, you get a chance to re-evaluate whether you really want to open the Dark Matter app, and that question makes all the difference in the world.

   d.   Use apps like Forest to minimise distractions in a digital form. This app plants a virtual seed, and you can see the tree grow for the time you have set. The tree starts to wither if you touch your screen before the set time. There is something compelling and satisfying in seeing even a virtual tree grow, and it kills us to see it wither. It sounds childish, but it is an amazingly impactful tool to drive focused, offline work.

Use the External Brain

Our brains have limited horsepower, and we have been trained since childhood to direct that energy to remember things. From remembering your partner's birthday to last quarter's numbers, from reciting error-free poems in the orals to verbatim information and definitions in the exams, the Indian education system and society have always placed immense importance on our remembering these details. The more you remember, the more glory you receive. The end result is an overburdened RAM with a lot of unnecessary data floating around.

If we intend to make the best use of our brain without getting hindered by societal expectations, we need to bring a behaviour and attitude change towards our obsession with remembering things. It is of minimal use for us to remember that London is the capital of the UK if this fact, in today's day and age, can be looked up on the internet in one second. I am not recommending that we stop teaching geography at schools, but we should focus more on giving kids a holistic understanding of London City, its culture, its history and economy instead of making them learn by rote and regurgitate its capital status in a quiz. As adults, with far more demands on our cognitive power, it makes good sense to release as much information from short-term or even long-term memory and rely on the wide variety of technological tools available to free up brain horsepower and concentrate it on something more productive and impactful. Hence, one good strategy is to unload as much information as possible and use the widely available tools to free up prime neuron space. Let's explore how.

1. *Use reminder apps*: No need to remember any appointment. Set up reminders on your phone for every single, even mildly important, event. From calling your mom on her birthday, wishing your partner on your anniversary, following up on a proposal shared with a client and dragging yourself to the grocery store, use the phone to remind you. The more you depend on your phone as your executive assistant, the more trust you will develop in your ability to schedule things, and the less your brain will worry about remembering them.

2. *Calendarise everything*: If it needs anything more than ten minutes, put the activity on your calendar, especially on a workday. Then follow your calendar like a child following a parent with blind trust. It creates a virtuous cycle. As you rely on your calendar more often, you will realise that you are spending your time

intentionally. You will then feel more satisfied and the quality of your life will improve. This behaviour will give you a dopamine hit of having spent time well, and you will crave this reward more and more. Some addictions are good, and getting addicted to one's calendar is the best of all.

3. *Take notes*: The following diagram beautifully captures learning as done with note-taking and without it. Whenever you find anything worth remembering, put it in your notes. If paper and pen are not your thing and you find it difficult to carry them everywhere, use your phone's notes apps. Don't trust your brain to remember anything. If you like it or want to remember it, note it down.

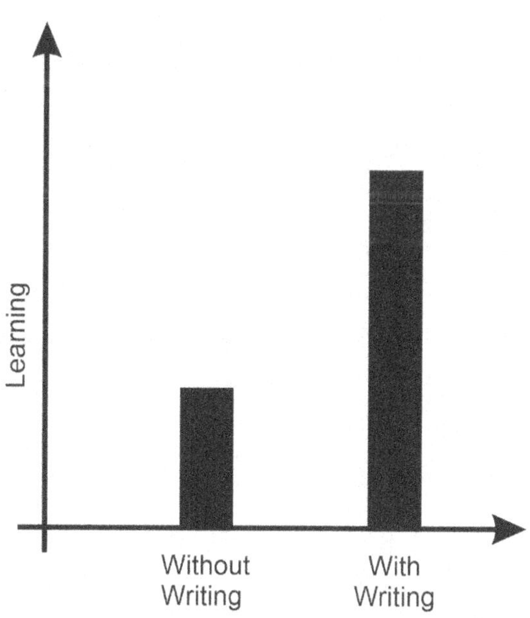

If we want to lead authentic, fulfilled, high-quality lives, our energy at the workplace needs to shine the brightest. To brighten your energy, use rituals that get you into that mood, help you escape the Dark Matter, like email and messages, and avoid multitasking. Focus on a single task in a carved-out time block, free of distractions. Break the doom loop of scrolling on phones by using the strategies mentioned above. At the same time, release valuable real estate in your brain by using technology for remembering things, taking notes and calendarising your schedule. Even with these techniques, a long workday with intense action can be very strenuous and tiring. In the next section, we will explore how to navigate Bright Energy depletion and strategies to recharge and take on the next day with Brightness.

- The evolution of technology has not necessarily made humans more productive.
- The tools available provide a fertile playground to our monkey mind to keep jumping between ideas with an overload of sensations that shatter our focus.
- Candid communication with your manager and senior stakeholders is the key to reclaiming time at the workplace. Some strategies you can use are:
    - Prepare thoroughly, with details on your work plan and possible issues.
    - Schedule a formal meeting to discuss your workload and your plan.
    - Present your Eisenhower matrix and discuss the priorities you have set.
    - Express commitment and build trust by delivering tasks as committed.
    - Publicly declare your Eisenhower matrix to your stakeholders to know your priorities and recalibrate their expectations.
- The plethora of meetings we have to attend are a major derailer of productivity.
- A good meeting flow can drive up the effectiveness of the meetings and help us use our time well:
    - Start with why. Explain the objective in the meeting invite itself.
    - Have a clear agenda outlined and shared.

- o Timebox the meeting with specified time for each topic.
  - o Have a clear outcome required from each section of the meeting.
  - o Recap key decisions taken, outcomes achieved and next steps and responsibilities.
- Emails are time-guzzlers, the enemies of focused, deep work and affect our relation with time negatively, leading to a surge in Dark Energy. Problems with email usage:
  - o Decision fatigue—every email received opens a can of decisions to be made
  - o Email wars—conversations that can go on to hundreds of emails being exchanged, with minimal output and massive ego destruction
  - o Immediate response expectations and blurring boundaries
  - o Context switching—this lets attention residue remain, and a return to an optimum focused state takes minimum of fifteen minutes after each interruption.
- The four types of email:
  - o The questions
  - o The conversations
  - o The broadcasts
  - o The administrative workload
- Calculate your email brightness index to know how are you engaging with this tool and what needs to improve.

- Solutions to the problem of email time hogging:
  - Carve out dedicated blocks of time by implementing email batching;
  - Avoid e-conversations; call instead;
  - Prioritise and declutter your inbox
  - Batch administrative emails
  - Establish and respect boundaries
- While technology has created the problems of time-guzzling tools like email and WhatsApp, it has also provided antidotes.
- Our phones are powerful devices that can trap us into a doom loop. We need to break out of it by:
  - Conducting an app audit
  - Organising our home screen
  - Managing notifications
  - Setting time limits for time-wasting, social media apps.
- Thanks to technology we need not remember everything. We can use technology as the second brain by:
  - Using reminder apps
  - Trusting and following the calendar and putting in every task that takes more than ten minutes
  - Writing down anything worth noting; this way, you needn't trust your memory to remember details.

Section 4
Recharging Time

Depleting Energies and Burnout

ONE OF THE HIGHEST ANXIETY-INDUCING EVENTS IN our lives these days is our phone battery dying. As much as 72 per cent of Indians, including me, experience increased anxiety if the phone battery goes below 20 per cent and we see the battery marker going red. But do we feel the same anxiety or even understand that our own Bright Energy battery is going below 20 per cent or is being completely depleted? Do we appreciate the signals our body and mind give when the energy battery starts to drain and reach depletion levels? Do we stop and reflect to recharge ourselves or give in to the culture of 'hustle on' or 'power through'?

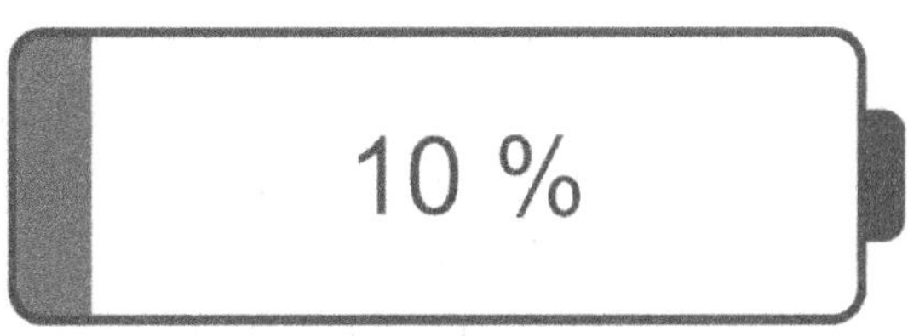

We started this journey of reclaiming time by understanding our body's relation to Bright and Dark energy. To be the best version of ourselves, we must learn about our Bright

Energy cycles and work with them. The more Bright Energy we generate, the better we operate, allowing us to use the time for the intended usage. The more our energy battery gets depleted and replaced by Dark Energy, the more damage occurs. Before we deep-dive into the pitfalls of Bright Energy depletion and its replacement with Dark Energy, let us revisit the brain and its connection with various cognitive abilities.

Previously, we discussed that the old brain, consisting of the limbic system of the amygdala, hippocampus and cerebellum, is the primitive part, a gift from the experiences of all our ancestors that controls all our involuntary and emotional functions, our fight-or-flight response and our deep-rooted habits and memory. The new brain, including the pre-frontal cortex, is the logic centre that controls our decision-making, imagination, thinking, planning and executive function activities. We also discussed that the brain guzzles about 20 per cent of the body's energy.

When our body is full of energy, the brain can smoothly manage energy flow to all its parts and functions. However, given that the body's energy is finite and the brain is its biggest user, it has to use it judiciously when resources start depleting. The functions being conducted by the old brain—the pumping of the heart, the functioning of the respiratory system and the absorption of energy through the digestive system are all vital functions. Diverting whatever limited energy is left to these parts of the brain thus becomes more critical, and this is what happens: the newer brain performs essential functions, no doubt, but not life-threatening if stopped. We all know many people whose logic centre seems not to be be getting any energy at all but who are happily gallivanting away!

So, with lower energy reserves, our new brain starts getting less and less fuel, and our cognitive function starts getting impaired. We feel exhausted, unable to focus, make sound decisions and process information in general. While the hustle culture pushes us to power through it all—to work for one more hour and finish that pending draft and only then take a break—we end up inflicting more damage, not only to our bodies and brain but also to the work we are doing in this exhausted state.

How many times have we had to completely redo the garbage work we did the day before, simply because it had been late and we tried to push through our exhaustion? Unlike phones, our bodies don't give us many alarming red signals of our battery going below 20 per cent, nor are we adept at reading them so we can start recharging it. Hence, we are mostly unaware of the signs of approaching burnout. Instead of putting ourselves to charge, we deplete it completely. Bouncing back from zero is much more difficult. Some signs can tell us that our Bright energy levels are dropping, and we can adopt the strategies mentioned below to start working on recharging ourselves.

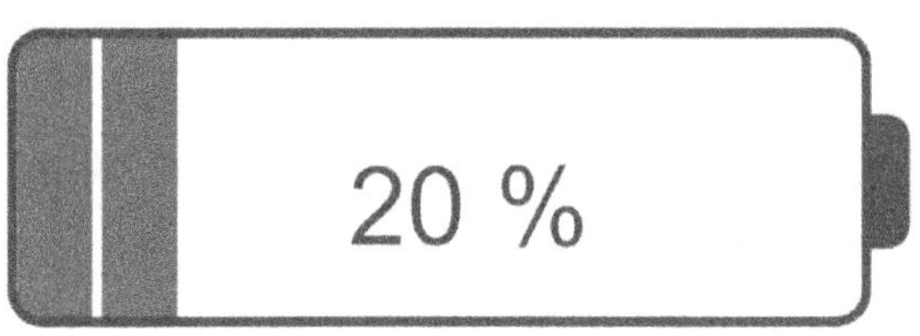

0 %

Signs of Approaching Burnout

1. *Frequent misses*: You are missing deadlines and meetings, making errors in submissions, mistakes in calculation, forgetting jobs allocated and struggling to complete tasks you once found easy.

2. *Reduced creativity*: You are unable to come up with new ideas or generate new approaches to solving problems. You feel a mental block restarting work on ongoing projects and are dreading starting anything new.

3. *Working without a break*: You eat at your desk, take no breaks, run from one meeting to the next and take back-to-back calls. You forget what a weekend feels like as you work through most of it. You are a machine, working nonstop on coffee and willpower.

4. *Negative attitude*: You are constantly dissatisfied with your work, your colleagues, your manager, the system and the world at large. You have deep cynicism about your role and the tasks assigned to you, and you find yourself complaining most of the time. You quickly lose your temper, and relations with your colleagues are strained as you constantly criticise them but can't take any constructive criticism.

5. *Withdrawal*: You have stopped liking the company and are withdrawing from team activities or even interactions with them. You are skipping lunches, skiving off social engagements with the team and literally jumping under the table to hide from HR (no team bonding activities, please!).

6. *Poorer performance and reduced sense of personal achievement*: You are seeing your performance go down. You are frequently being clubbed with the non-performers, and your identity feels shaken. You feel you are not contributing enough and feel no sense of achievement. You don't find the work meaningful and start dreading coming to the office.

If even one of the symptoms listed above holds true for you, your Dark Energy is on the rise, and it is only a matter of time before you pass over to the dark side, Mr Frodo! Your relationship with time has gone for a toss, and you feel you have lost control. It is crucial to step back now, reflect and actively start working towards recharging your Bright Energy battery. Bright Energy rituals can help us break this Dark Energy cycle. But the most effective strategy to recharge our batteries is to disconnect, to give our brain time and a chance to recover.

Our brains today are constantly stimulated by one thing or the other, one screen or the other, from the moment we wake up to the time we go to sleep, exhausted. The first step towards recovering our charge is to reduce this stimulation. We are on a constant dopamine high and crave stimulation from new content on our phones and emails. When we remove these stimuli, the mind comes to a less excited state that we call boredom.

Embrace boredom.

We tend to fear boredom and will do everything we can to escape it; it is an uncomfortable void we feel we must fill at all costs. In truth, boredom serves an essential, fundamental purpose. It serves as the catalyst for cognitive rejuvenation, boosting our creativity and recharging our batteries as our mind wanders, without distraction or specific objective. In J.R.R. Tolkein's words, 'Not all who wander are lost.' When we let our minds wander without the crutch of constant stimuli, we create space for innovation and problem-solving.

Research says that thoughts rise unbidden when our minds relax.[13] Of all such instances, only 12 per cent of the time are we thinking about past occurrences. About 28 per cent of the time, we think about what we are grappling with at present. An astounding 48 per cent of the time, more than the past and present combined, our wandering mind thinks about the future. How often has it happened that you have found yourself planning your day while in the shower? Do solutions to problems you have been working on suddenly spring to you when you are on a walk? This is the power of the wandering mind when it is away from constant stimuli. Embracing boredom is giving your mind

---

13   Chris Bailey, 'Stop Being 'So Busy': The Psychology behind Why Being Lazy Is Actually Good for Your Brain', *Make It*, 19 May 2020, https://www.cnbc.com/2020/05/19/stop-being-busy-psychology-behind-why-being-lazy-is-actually-good-for-your-brain.html.

that chance to reboot and engage in more profound and meaningful thinking.

Along with embracing boredom, also work on disconnecting. As explained earlier, residual attention is a massive overhead we carry as we move from one task to the other. Imagine adding some weights to your head as you start the day and gradually adding more. By the time we reach the close of the day, this cluster of weights reaches a significant load. For our sustained mental health, it becomes imperative that we offload this residue.

In this interconnected world, where we are available 24x7 to our colleagues and managers, it becomes difficult to establish boundaries. Even if you love your job passionately and dream about working on the next challenging project, your body and brain have a limit. Once close to depletion, you have no choice but to actively work on replenishing your energy reserves. Disconnecting from work is an essential step to do that.

The EOD Ritual

A good way to disconnect from work is to deploy the Zeigarnik effect. The Zeigarnik effect is the cause of attention residue but can also be the remedy. To recap, the effect states that the mind holds information about an unfinished task in its active memory, in its RAM. Because of this, even when we have finished our day, we feel our mind buzzing with the workload; information on what we could not finish today, and what we have to tackle the next day.

An excellent method to stop this buzzing is to have an end-of-the-day ritual.

A good end of the workday ritual does a few things:

1. Lets you summarise the day—how it went, what you accomplished
2. Enables you to plan the next day in a nutshell
3. Signals to your mind that the workday is over and helps release the information it is carrying.

Just five minutes of an end-of-day ritual can add a lot of value to the quality of your life after work. I explain below how I approach this ritual.

1. I open my Outlook calendar and quickly jot down the key wins of the day in my notebook. These can be very small ones or huge victories; it doesn't matter. What were the top three or four wins of my day? What were some key decisions I made?
2. I open the calendar for the next day and see if any urgent submissions are pending. If there is a meeting I have not prepared for, I note down the three big rocks for the next day, preferably to be finished in the first half.
3. With these two actions, I feel I gave my best today and feel well-prepared to tackle the next day. To add some flourish, as recommended by many experts like Cal Newport, I utter my personal catchphrase. This may sound funny or childish, but I have followed this advice and found it has immense power. I close my laptop and say, 'Chalo, that's done for the day!'

The phrase is the most essential part of the ritual. It signals to my brain to release the information stored and the attention residue of the whole day, and get ready for some relaxation and unwinding at home. That anticipation of how I will now spend the next few hours working on myself by reading or listening to podcasts or spending time with my loved ones releases the happiness hormone. I also feel the entire residue seeping off my brain, instantly giving me a feeling of lightness. This deliberate practice helps me acknowledge the closure of my professional responsibilities and transition to a more relaxed state of mind.

Bright Exercise: Write your EOD Ritual

Steps you will take to signal the close of workday:

1. ____

2. ____

3. ____

Your personal catchphrase to signal to your brain that the day is done:

____

Our brain is a muscle. It needs both exercise and periods of relaxation to recover and recharge. After a high-intensity workday, rituals like this help start the recovery. The most important part of the brain's recovery is good sleep. Our chapter on Bright Energy discussed how sleep is the foundation of a good quality of life. To improve our relationship with time, we must give our body the necessary seven to eight hours of sleep.

Strategies like a digital detox, a disconnection from technology and apps like WhatsApp and Outlook, and a reduction in our overall screen time are necessary steps to improve the quality of our personal lives. We need to unplug from technology to relax and recharge our cave-dweller brain, which is not adept at handling continuous exposure to so many stimuli. This detox is the best form of self-care and self-discipline that will pay you many times over as you move on with life. With good sleep and a recharged brain, we can wake up each day reinvigorated, full of Bright Energy and committed to taking charge of our limited time here on Earth.

To make the most of this toolkit, try all the experiments we have discussed in the previous sections. With these explorations, you should be able to create an ideal day catalogue of your Bright Stars and methods to harness your Bright Energy. You should be able to understand what distracts you and what helps you keep your focus sharp during important time blocks. You should be able to create your own rejuvenation rituals that help charge your Bright Energy batteries to take up the next day's demands.

I have charted out my ideal day catalogue below. I have arrived at it with some experimentation and attempt to follow this regularly. Create your own versions and see how your Bright Energy rises and wanes through the day. With well-harnessed Bright Energy, sharp focus and conscious intention, you should have all the tools to be your best, most productive and—most importantly—happiest self.

Ideal Day Catalogue					
Time	Activity	Focus Type	Details	Duration (minutes)	Bright Energy
6.00–6.30 a.m.	Wake-up routine	Routine	Morning routine: Brush teeth and get ready	30	0
6.30–7.15 a.m.	Gym	Health	Light workout and yoga	45	3
7.15–7.45 a.m.	Morning tea	Routine	Have tea with my partner and chat	30	3
7.45–8.00 a.m.	Shower	Routine	Daily ablutions	15	3
8.00–8.30 a.m.	Sitar practice	Passion	Practise on the sitar— Personal Bright Star	30	4
8.30–8.45 a.m.	Getting ready	Routine	Get ready for the office	15	4

Ideal Day Catalogue					
Time	Activity	Focus Type	Details	Duration (minutes)	Bright Energy
8.45–9.30 a.m.	Travel to the office	Travel	Travel to the office, read a book or listen to a podcast on the way	45	3
Before Office Time					
9.30–11.00 a.m.	Focused work block 1	Bright Work	Focus on critical tasks or high-priority projects—Bright Star at work	85	4
			Break—desk yoga	5	4
11.00–11.15 a.m.	Email batching	Administrative work	Check and respond to emails, clear inbox	15	3
11.15–11.30 p.m.	Workout break	Break	Take a walk around the office, stretch and do some desk exercises	15	4
11.30–12.45	Focused work		Continue working on complex tasks	70	4

Ideal Day Catalogue					
Time	Activity	Focus Type	Details	Duration (minutes)	Bright Energy
12.45–1.00 p.m.	Mid-day review	Reflecting/ planning	Review progress made so far; plan tasks for the afternoon	15	3
1.00–2.00 p.m.	Lunch break	Break	Take a full break for lunch, relaxation, recharge	60	4
2.00–3.30 p.m.	Focused work block 3		Focus on creative or strategic tasks	85	4
		Bright Work	Break—desk yoga	5	4
3.30–3.45 p.m.	Email batching	Administrative work	Check and respond to emails, clear inbox	15	3
3.45–4.00 p.m.	Administrative tasks	Administrative work	Handle admin tasks like reports, minor planning or scheduling	15	2
4.00–4.15 p.m.	Snack break	Break	Eat some healthy snack, talk to colleagues	15	3

Ideal Day Catalogue					
Time	Activity	Focus Type	Details	Duration (minutes)	Bright Energy
4.15–5.30 p.m.	Focused work block 4	Bright Work	Focus on key deliverables for the next day	70	3
			Break—listen to music	5	3
5.30–5.40 p.m.	Final email batching	Administrative work	Quick check and clear inbox for the day	10	3
5.40–5.55 p.m.	Final review and work wrap-up	Reflecting/ planning	Review accomplishments of the day; assess remaining tasks	15	3
5.55–6.00 p.m.	End of day ritual	Bright Work	Tidy up workspace, set intentions for the next day	5	4
After Office Time					
6.00–7.00 p.m.	Commute home	Travel	Listen to a podcast	60	3

Ideal Day Catalogue					
Time	Activity	Focus Type	Details	Duration (minutes)	Bright Energy
7.00–8.00 p.m.	Relax at home	Rejuvenation	Play with dog, hang out with parents, watch TV	60	4
8.00–9.00 p.m.	Sitar practice	Passion	Practise on the sitar	60	3
9.00–10.00 p.m.	Dinner	Routine	Have dinner with my partner	60	4
10.00–11.00 p.m.	Night-time routine	Routine	Watch TV, read a book	60	3

Bright Energy

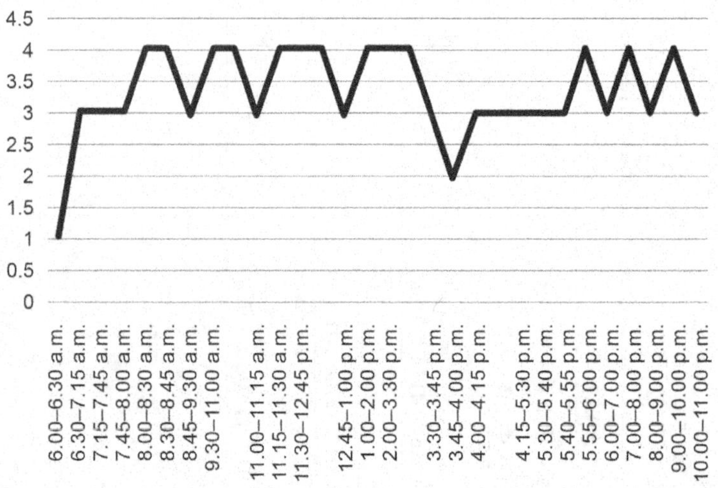

- Understanding our Bright Energy cycle is the most important step to reclaiming and recharging our time.
- Unlike our phones, our body's signals are subtle when it approaches depletion or burnout. The signs indicate a surge of Dark Energy and include:
  - Frequent misses: Missing deadlines, submissions, errors in calculations and other mistakes
  - Reduced creativity: Unable to come up with new ideas, new approaches to problem-solving
  - Working without a break: Having back-to-back meetings, becoming a machine working on coffee and willpower
  - Negative attitude: Constant dissatisfaction with work, colleagues, manager, HR and the world at large
  - Withdrawal: From team activities, socialisation and company
  - Reduced sense of achievement: Being clubbed with non-performers, not finding work meaningful and dreading coming to the office.
- The first step to recover from the overdrive of the monkey mind is to reduce the stimulation we receive from phones and emails and embrace boredom.
- The second step is to disconnect, create boundaries and fiercely protect recharging your batteries.
- Use the Zeigarnik effect to your advantage with an EOD ritual.

Conclusion: Becoming One with Time

WE STARTED EXPLORING THE RELATIONSHIP BETWEEN time, energy, and purpose with a simple question: why do we want more time? Our experiments to answer this question will lead us to understand ourselves first. On multiple time scales—from the very next moment to the length of our lifetime—these experiments help us fathom what we want to do with our time on Earth. They lead us to even more questions about our purpose, the impact we want to create and the legacy we want to build.

The clarity of purpose becomes the anchor for further exploration. Perhaps we now understand that life is not about finding more time but about being intentional with it, about performing actions that help us take the next steps towards our purpose. We need to align our existence, actions and choices with this core that gives life meaning. When we operate with our purpose as our North Star, time ceases to become something you can have or not have—it ceases to become a perpetually elusive concept. It becomes a partner in realising that purpose; it gives us the power of intention, which helps us direct our time most effectively.

To translate our purpose into actions, we need to understand the system that makes it possible for us to do anything at all. The Bright and Dark Energy batteries power us and create Bright and Dark Matter. To manage our time, we first need to manage our energies better. You might have all the time in the world, but you cannot use it effectively if you don't have the energy to do what you intended. With the experiments in this book, I urge you to understand your energy cycles and reflect on when you find your day brightest and when the dark clouds appear.

Armed with an understanding of our body's energy rhythms, we can address why we are not happy with the time we do have, what we are doing with our time at present, why we procrastinate, and why we are not starting the important project we need to submit. To start the journey of coming out of our comfort zone, we need to ask these uncomfortable questions.

The various experiments help us understand the causes of our inertia and try to overcome this procrastination. Try all of them and see what works for you. We are all wired differently, and no panacea exists. These simple protocols need just a few moments for you to set but provide enormous clarity for the time ahead. Overcome procrastination one day, one hour, one moment at a time. Focus on taking the first step, and the rest will follow. Fix your Bright Star every day and see your day brighten up.

An essential step in transforming from unaware bystanders to active owners of our lives and our time is to learn to answer the question, 'What matters to me?' If we are clear about our purpose and understand the energy rhythms of our bodies, answering this with certainty becomes easier. To lead a quality life, we need to work on nurturing our Bright Energy batteries. Prioritise work that provides you a boost in Bright Energy and also rewards you with growth, both financially and personally. Get your priorities right!

Once you are clear about your priorities, the next important step is to work on them with complete focus. In a world filled with Dark Matter, with screens, reels and messaging apps all vying for our attention, even the best-laid plans will fall flat without focus. Our natural inclination to multitask can be a significant derailer. To work with focus, we need to understand how to focus.

We need to understand the inner workings of the old and the new brain and their functions, to understand what goes inside our brain when we try to focus. We touched upon the various hormones and the purpose they fulfill in focusing and refocusing. With this knowledge, we explored multiple techniques to increase focus consistently and remove distractions. Focusing on one task at a time, we make the most of every moment.

Translating these strategies to the workplace requires moving beyond simply reflecting on it. Time is a particularly precious resource at the workplace and is often wasted through Dark Matter, such as emails, unplanned meetings, messages and miscommunication. The practical strategies we have discussed help reclaim time by setting boundaries, improving communication, using tools like calendar time blocks efficiently and deploying methods to escape the email Dark Matter rabbit hole. We should focus on creating an environment that allows us to do our best, focused work free from the constant pull of distractions.

Lastly, we need to know when to recharge our Bright Energy batteries. Disconnect and allow them time to recover to bring our brain muscles back to performing at maximum potential levels. Create your own disconnection rituals to signal the start of the recovery phase to your mind. Embrace boredom and let your mind to wander. Sleep adequately, in line with your circadian rhythms, and provide the brain with the required recovery time. A recharged brain is the best ally to take on each day and use that time to the best of your abilities.

In the end, I want to recall the formula we discussed for being productive.

$$\text{Productivity} = \text{Time spent} \times \text{Focus} \times \text{Bright Energy} = \text{Bright Work}$$

If, through the experiments and protocols in this toolkit, you are able to arrive at your Bright Energy patterns, understand how to improve and nurture your Bright Energy and work with focus in a deep state of flow. By spending time in the manner you had planned, you will find immense satisfaction and contentment. Productivity is not about hustle culture or working yourself to burnout—it is about making an informed choice on what you want to do at any given moment and then doing it. It is work that creates Brightness in your life. You will end each day feeling productive and content that you have lived your day well. What is life but a continuum of days well lived?

At the close, I want to recall what we established at the outset: this book aims not to create more time for you but to make you understand that 'you are time'. Every moment you experience, the decision you make, the emotion you feel is time expressing itself through you. Time is not a separate entity; it is not something to catch up with, race against, master or manage in isolation. It is important to differentiate between time and a clock. A clock is just a crutch to measure 'world time'. It is not time itself. Time is the life you choose to live in that moment. Time is you making those irreversible decisions that define who your authentic self is. Time is you, and you are time.

We stop feeling rushed, enslaved and powerless when we truly understand this. Living free and living with intention is one and the same. It is realising that every moment offers us a choice—a choice to spend that moment doing what matters to us. We can either live reactively, flowing unaware like flotsam in this passage of time, or live retrospectively, thrashing against it trying to remember the good old days, or live actively. We can be active architects of our life, take control, align our actions to our purpose and flow with time rather than against it. A life well-lived is not about its length but one where each moment is filled with meaning, where each moment lived is a conscious choice. Find these moments and make the choice that aligns with your purpose. Choose quality over quantity, depth over speed and the richness of experience over material riches.

This shift in mindset—from having time to being time— changes everything. It reframes the stress of not having enough hours in the day and externalising our fate to an unjust world to give us a choice on our priorities, purpose and how we live. When you are time yourself, how can you ever run out of it? You are the present; you are making deliberate choices that reflect your values, align with your purpose and define who you are.

Lived like this, life becomes more than just a series of tasks and checkboxes. It transforms into something richer—where our time, energy, focus and purpose are in harmony. To live a Bright Life isn't to simply manage time—it's to live better. To live with authenticity. To experience time not as something to chase but as life itself—flowing through its moments with intention, presence and a sense of aliveness. Life is not just about being productive; it's about feeling deeply fulfilled; a life that is enriched—*a Bright Life*.

The upcoming books in the **Bright Life Toolkit Series** are designed to help you on this journey. They'll offer insights for deeper self-discovery and equip you with the tools to become your most authentic self—while nurturing stronger, more meaningful relationships. As you move towards building your own Bright Life, experiment with the tools in this Time Energy Toolkit, harness your Bright Energy and remember: *you are time, and time is you.*

Acknowledgements

The Time Energy Toolkit is the result of countless people who have helped me design my days, harness my energy and honour my time with intention.

First and foremost, to my partner Manoj—thank you for giving me the confidence to put myself out there; the courage to be seen, to share, and to leap despite my fears, knowing you would be there to steady and embrace me. You are my anchor, my fixed point in the universe. All I want from time is more of it with you.

To my parents, Deepa and Shyam Sunder Khare—thank you for the most loving and nurturing childhood. Your teachings and values are the foundation of the ideas in this book. Manoj and I are building our lives in the light of your example.

To my sister Tina—growing up with you was pure joy. Thank you for being my champion through every season of life, from supporting me when I was coming out to helping shape the early drafts of this book.

To our dearly departed dog Vichy—the way you lived your short life, with joy and abandon, is the very definition of living your time well. Yours was a bright, beautiful life, and we love and miss you deeply.

This book would not have been possible without the encouragement of my extended family, friends and colleagues at Godrej. To Nisa and Pirojsha Godrej, thank you for leading with purpose and authenticity, and for instilling in me the belief that when we do good for people and planet, we create lasting impact.

To my life coaches, Gaurav Pandey, Sumit Mitra, Megha Goel, Subhasish Pattanaik, Lalit Makhijani and Vandana Scolt—from you I have learnt not only excellence at the workplace, but also how to be a better human being. Your belief, wisdom and encouragement shaped both this book and the Bright Life it stands for.

To my brilliant team—Shreeram Joshi, Duke Pande, Supriya Naik, Prathamesh Gharge, Lavanya Gupta, Harshita Tiwari, Dimple Choudhary and Parag Arora—thank you for being the foundation of all that I do. I couldn't ask for a better team to journey with.

To Aurodeep, my editor, and everyone at Westland— thank you for helping bring this project to life. Your generous partnership and editorial wisdom shaped this book, and the Bright Life series owes its start to you.

Lastly, to you, dear reader. If you've followed my newsletter *The Foundation Project*, thank you for your companionship, suggestions and support. You are gifting me your most precious resource: your time. That is the greatest honour. If this book brings even a little more brightness to your life, I'll be deeply grateful.

The tables and exercises in the book can be downloaded as an editable Excel sheet from this link. Use them well.

www.ingramcontent.com/pod-product-compliance
Lightning Source LLC
Chambersburg PA
CBHW060907140726
47996CB00001B/155